Kick Start
the Broomstick

Kick Start
the Broomstick

ANGIE K. BARNETT

Matador
9 Priory Business Park, Wistow Road
Kibworth Beauchamp
Leicester LE8 0RX, UK
Tel: (+44) 116 279 2299
Fax: (+44) 116 279 2277
Email: books@troubador.co.uk
Web: www.troubador.co.uk/matador

ISBN 978 1780880 549

British Library Cataloguing in Publication Data.
A catalogue record for this book is available from the British Library.

Typeset in 11pt Adobe Garamond Pro by Troubador Publishing Ltd, Leicester, UK

Matador is an imprint of Troubador Publishing Ltd

Printed and bound in the UK by TJ International, Padstow, Cornwall

To Nanna O'Conner for passing on the Psychic gift with pride and for guiding me on the right path throughout my life.

My parents whom without you none of this would be possible. Thank you for always believing in me no matter what, but most of all your love, support and encouragement has helped make me who I am today.

My sisters, my best friends. The 'Power of 3'. All that's left to say is 'We did it'.

And finally, to the inner strength in me....
'THANKS FOR NEVER GIVING UP!

CONTENTS

PREFACE

The TV was on, mum had just rushed through the door from work, barely taken her coat off and was already in the kitchen as usual making tea and Dad was still at work. We were all pretty much doing the same thing as what we do every day after just getting in from school. My brother Terry was watching cartoons, his favorite thing to do, I was playing house as a young girl would simply getting on everybody's nerves copying my mum in the kitchen with her yelling 'will you get out from underneath my feet or your going to get burnt'! My sisters Donna and Allison were upstairs planning their outfit so that they could eat and run straight out the door afterwards with the music blaring and nothing but gossip oozing out of our bedroom. Curious, I sat on the edge of the bed listening to the banter but as always the conversation stopped as soon as they noticed my presence. Instead I'm sat watching Donna apply her make-up, she was so gifted and always looked so pretty as did Allison but Donna was the creative one; freaky if you will, she always tried to be different but truly did have a talent at doing just that.

Anyway, it was a really cold night and the wind had started to pick up. The nights were drawing near as it was almost coming peak into winter. Then through the bellowing sound of the music we could hear

KICK START THE BROOMSTICK

the phone ring, we all dive for it because at this stage it was still a novelty to us as a family, we were all pretty much obsessed with it! Terry beat us all to the phone, answered it downstairs then called out 'Mam, Nanna O'Conner is on the phone'. My sisters and me just stopped what we were doing and just simply stared at each other waiting with bated breath at the outcome of the phone call. Our bedroom window was slightly ajar and the curtain blew wide almost hitting the light shade on the ceiling. We ran to the top of the stairs to try and listen in on the call, all we can hear is mum whispering to my Nan, she hung up the phone and shouted up the stairs to Donna the eldest as we run back into the bedroom so that she doesn't think we were listening 'watch the babies for me, I have to go see Nanna straight away'. Now, by the look on each other's faces and the upside down butterflies we experienced in our tummy; we knew this could only mean one thing. Nanna had a message for Mammy, only who was it from? Who was it for? What was the message about? The three of us girls sat on our beds taking bets on who we thought it was for. Donna thought it was for her, something in regards to her being naughty at school. Allison and me burst out laughing. Allison thought it was about her, maybe Nanna had seen her Prince Charming, and then I thought it was about me and that I would be a famous movie star or something. After all, I was only 10 at the time. No. Instantly we knew it wasn't about us so then we all sat on Donna's bed and wracked our brains on who could have possibly done something to hurt the family in anyway? We linked pinky fingers & said 'Power of 3, come to me, show us a vision of who it is thee' then instantly we absolutely got spooked at the thought of what Karma/Spell they were about to receive from Nanna; that and the electric shock we received from each other as we pulled our fingers away!

Preface

The three of us all at the same time smiled and whispered out loud those famous words 'the night is still young and you are still beautiful my darling'...

And so the story begins....

CHAPTER 1

The Original Witch of Chriswick

You see growing up in our family wasn't quite what some people would consider normal. I know, I hear you all say 'what is normal', Nanna's baking cakes, buying you sweets etc, and the cuddly type right? Well Nanna O'Conner was all of that and more. The best way to describe her is she was a large personality in a very small package. 5'2" tall, kind of full figured with quite a large chest. Her hair was a mousy brown color and even at 60 years of age she had very few grey hairs. Her hair was so very thick and always looked adorable. I always remember her having a hanky up her sleeve. She would never use paper tissues, she always used material ones and hers were always embroidered beautifully with either flowers or her initials on them. Nanna truly was ever so glamorous, her nails, make-up and clothes were always immaculate, you would never see her unpolished, even on a Sunday she would still look lovely in her cooking apron over her clothes. She would make the best roast potatoes I've ever tasted in my entire life with her Sunday Dinner. For those of you who are not familiar with British traditions the majority of homes in the UK on Sunday's all cook a feast as big as Thanksgiving in the US. Nanna would make homemade rice pudding with the skin still on the top for after's, that's desert for the non Welsh people reading this, or she would have the three tier cake tray with all the French Fancies and Mint Viscount Biscuits. She would always have a cupboard filled with the best goodies and her personal favorites, a bag of mint imperials and a bowl of Pears on hand at the table next to her favorite chair in the living room.

Nanna's house always smelt of Imperial Leather Soap and Bryl Cream that my Bampie used to put on his hair. She even had a cover for the back of his chair so that it wouldn't ruin it! She had many little personal traits. Whenever any of us were sick as a child, without fail we knew Nanna would come around with a bottle of Lucozade with the crinkly plastic transparent orange paper wrapped around it and a bag of Orange's. This was a sign that we must REALLY be sick. Talking of plastic crinkly things, on Christmas Day every year, Nanna used to dress up as Father Christmas and walk around to each of the family homes and deliver our gifts. We were so excited hoping our house would be first. All the kids in the street used to love it and follow her house to house until they had to go home. Boy, if only she knew how much these special moments left lasting impressions on our hearts to this day. The really sad thing is that she worked really hard as a domestic cleaner in one of the Universities in Swansea right up until her retirement only she didn't get to enjoy it, she passed away not long after; which was such a shame as her and Bampie never got to enjoy their retirement together.

My Bampie was devastated after her death so much so that he turned into a complete recluse. He had two dogs, one after the other both named Bob. Go figure? They were identical dogs that my cousin had bought for him to help keep him company. It was so sad to see him deteriorate, he was always such a smart man and took great pride in himself yet here we are watching this frail man slip away before our eyes. They met through my Nanna's brother uncle Sid. Uncle Sid's house in Marsden Street Swansea was the local meeting point for what we would consider a gang of friends today and went on their very first date with my uncle's permission to the Tower Ballroom, a local dance hall in a place called Townhill, a small suburb in Swansea. They met, they danced; they fell in love and married one year later in 1946; dad was only 18 months old at the time. You see she lost my real Bampie in the war, my dad's father. My dad used to share stories with us about Bampie when he's come home late drunk from the pub. Without fail he would always find stray dogs, tie his tie around their neck and bring them home. My Nanna would get up and find some flea bitten mutt sitting on her kitchen floor and she would scream with the loudest scream 'Willie, get down here and see to this lodger you brought home'. Of course Bampie can't even remember bringing a dog home but would run like hell out of the house to stop Nanna hitting him over the head with the T-Towel! We would just belly laugh as Dad shared the stories.

After my Nan passed away I always visited him during my trips to Wales. I would sit on the sofa and he would look me in the eyes and fill up with tears and say 'Angela, you are the spit out of your Nanna's mouth do you know that'? It was a lovely thing to hear; I guess I did follow her in more than many ways. She was always so elegant and always smelt of Alysha Ashley – Mostly Musk perfume. I remember when she first fell ill with a stroke; I used to take my heated gas hairbrush to the hospital and curl her hair. She loved that I did that and bought me a huge cane chair for my bedroom in the attic as a 'thank you'. Oh boy I loved that chair. I actually made a cushion for it in Dress and Design class in school and dressed it with allsorts of colored pins and ribbons. Unfortunately the chair was thrown out when my parents sold the house in Torrington Road, a house in which we had lived since I was six in a local community area called Gendros in Swansea, South Wales! Now, the attic was a different story. You see, whilst the attic was being renovated for me I went to stay at Nanna's. My dad and Bampie did the work themselves. Dad fell through the ceiling twice, oooops, that was the funniest thing. My dad isn't the quietest person on the planet either so you could hear him screaming from half way up the street. Baring in mind Nanna also only lived about fifteen houses away in the next street and you could see the attic window from her back garden, you could also hear him from there! She always teased my dad and told him to put a phone in there for me. I was actually banned from using the phone as I'd always run the bills sky high and when my mum was in Australia on vacation one time the phone bill was astronomical and I got the blame so as you can imagine; dad did not find that funny at all.

I loved everything about my grand parents house; everything had a story. It was quite eccentric if you will but everything had its place from the old tea trolley to the photos of all us grandchildren. The living room was ever so cozy and she had the prettiest paintings of Fairies on he wall above the fireplace that I swear used to watch you as you walked about the room and as my gift grew the more in tune I became with the fairies. The dining room was where she had her 'Witchy Cupboard'; all of her things she used to practice were kept inside this cupboard. She kept them hidden in material so that Bampie wouldn't suspect anything. I also years after moving to America started to develop my very own 'Witchy Cupboard' that only got shown to the very few! Her kitchen believe it or not was actually quite old fashioned, basic countertops, basic table and sliding door cupboard above on the wall. She always had matching sugar and milk bowls 'Just incase You Get Visitors', she used to say! The hallway had this three dimensional picture of Jesus on the wall, to protect all who entered her home. You couldn't miss this; it was directly in front of you to the left hand side of the kitchen door. The upstairs contained something very, very magical. The Music Jewelry Box. This box has played a great influence to me and my sisters; which you will learn but it plays the theme song from Mary Poppins 'Chim Chimney Chim Chimney Chim Chim Charoo'. This box would go off on it's own so many times, even with the lid down. You see it was designed to look like one of that very old Gram's that was built to play records. So many weird and wonderful things happened in the month that I stayed there, especially with the box, it would light up when you passed the bedroom, bare in mind there was no light fixture or built in electrics to it at all but when my Nanna was alive, she always advised us girls that when she needed us to be aware of something or wanted to forewarn us as the 'Power of Three', no matter what we would be doing, if we heard that noise we had to meet to allow the powers that be provide us with the information. Lots more on this mysterious yet fascinating little treasure chest to come later in the story.

The house was always cold due to the fact she never had central heating at the time so she used to put me in the box room, the smallest bedroom in the house but the warmest with two massive quilts on the bed and lo and behold, not long after I'd climb into bed the fun would begin. The room would suddenly begin to get really cold and then all of a sudden a mist would form at the end of the bed, I would be absolutely petrified and hide under the quilt but would peep out every few seconds to see if they were still there and would watch the mist move about the room until eventually I would drop off to sleep. The next morning Nanna would be up before me and have a cooked breakfast of eggs, bacon and toast sitting on the table waiting for me and as soon as I walked into the kitchen, there she's be stood, in her nightgown, no teeth in as they'd be soaking in a glass of Steradent on the bathroom window sill and say 'you don't need to say a word, I know they were with you last night, they were just checking up on you and remember my darling, it's the living you have to be afraid of not the dead'. Then over breakfast we would discuss what my experience was, how I felt etc. This went on night after night during my length of stay with her. This I have to say was my first experience of being in the presence of spirits and yet every morning I would have something new to tell her. What's truly interesting about this story is after she passed away, the spirits often visited me in my attic bedroom at my parents house on Torrington Road only you'll learn more of that later in the story.

As you can see she was actually quite normal, well, to the world at least, only as soon as the front door was closed that was when she turned into 'The Original Witch of Chriswick'!!! She had to be really careful when she used her gift though because Bampie didn't agree with or like any of the things she did so she had to hide so much from him. He used to call it 'Hocus Pocus and Iddly Piddly Rubbish'. Amongst many things, which you'll learn on this journey with us she practiced Fortune Telling with the Crystal Ball, regular playing cards and Tea Leaves. Every Sunday I would go around to see her and ask her to bring out the Crystal Ball only we would have to wait for Bampie to go to bed after having his lunch first. It wouldn't take him long to drop off to sleep, you see, he'd been to the pub for a few pints before his lunch. Then the TV would go off, the magic little ball would come out of its hiding place into Nanna's hands. She would wipe it with the velvet cover and pass it to me so that my fingerprints would go over it, take it back and just stare into it and predict my future. I'm sure she did it as entertainment for a while as I was probably way too young to truly have that much ahead of me but if the truth were known I was just simply intrigued. It almost became addictive to me. I just wanted to hear the stories but she would always know how far to go with me without scaring me or getting herself into trouble with my dad for 'Feeding me with that rubbish'.

You see, one thing you need to know here is that as children we didn't know my Dad had the gift until years later, so we weren't surprised by his response to everything only we will go more depth with his story in the next chapter! I can't say I was surprised to learn about dad; after all, it's very rare things or family traits miss a generation?

It wasn't just the Fortune Telling that went on in Nanna's house that I was drawn to, it was the spirits she had living there. I can remember sitting on the sofa and the partition door opening and closing on its own, not truly thinking anything's wrong. Ten minutes later the same thing would happen again, only this time she turned to me and said 'it's O.K love, they just don't like what's on TV that's all. You would walk into her house at any given time of day and catch her talking out loud to them or if you were lucky enough to sleep over there as I spoke of earlier, you might actually even get a glimpse of them, or sense them around you at least. Nanna always believed they protected her.

The other thing would be her special Spells; she always had a solution for every ailment, removal of warts, etc. She would bury some raw bacon in the garden after rubbing it onto your wart first, then she would tie horse hair around it and cover it with a plaster until it fell off whilst under her breathe she would be whispering her own words to speed up the process. If any of us had chilblain's on our hands or feet from the cold weather she would make us urinate in a bucket and place our hands or feet into the urine; which was gross but it worked! There would always be someone knocking on her door to ask for help or a cure on some sort of ailment. I couldn't wait to go home and tell my mum everything that happened during my visits, what she'd predicted for me, everything. I don't think my feet hit the ground on the way home, let's just say I felt as if I was on that baby broomstick and I was gone with a million thoughts of excitement racing through my tiny little head at the same time, wondering mostly when it would be my turn to experience the gift. As Nanna always told me 'the seasons don't rush for nobody and when your time is right you will know'.

There was one slight problem with this picture though, in those days you weren't allowed to speak about your spiritual gifts or experiences for fear of people thinking you were nuts and belonged in the 'Luni Bin' or better known as Asylum. So unfortunately I had to keep my excitement to myself. I'd be laid in bed thinking about all the wonderful things I had to come in the future and how exciting the next time would be that I would enter my Nanna's house but mum always reminded me to keep the information to myself for now. I guess your probably thinking how unusual it was for me to be the youngest child being more excited by it? Not really, I guess I was always the curious one, always wanting to know the ins and outs of a cats backside if you will, only we were not allowed to be privy to all that went on in Nanna's house. So much was done behind the closed doors with the grown ups, we used to try and peep through the gap in the door or stand so close to the door so that we could hear what was being said and done but we'd almost always get caught and run like hell before they could see who it was that was there. All we could hear was the kitchen knife being stabbed into the raw chicken, several names being spoken out loud, strange smells and odd vibrations floating with the lights flickering, the famous words 'BUGS and FLEAS, BUGS and FLEAS, BUGS and FLEAS'. and then silence..the deed was done, only to WHOM? Nanna always added BUGS and FLEAS to any of her spells; I guess this was her own signature touch, one that we still repeat to this day believe it or not! As she walked out of the kitchen she would shout on the top of her voice 'if anyone else does anything to hurt you then I'll put the 'GYP' on him or her too'. Gyp was short for 'Gypsy Spell'; again, we still use this term today but in a nutshell it's what we call the 'Natural Spell' that we make happen with our thoughts alone and so as the famous saying goes 'Be careful what you wish for because it might just come true'. Nanna always reminded us of this when we were first learning to practice and for obvious reasons!

On the way home, we would pester our mum to share the exciting things that went on in the room where us children were not allowed but dad would just give mum one look and that would be the end of the conversation.

CHAPTER 2

The Seventh Son of the Seventh Son

My dad. Oh boy? How could I best describe him to you so that you get a clear picture of how he looks? He's 5.2" tall, and if I'm completely honest with you looks exactly like "Uncle Fester" from the Adams Family! He's balding, round bellied and wears his glasses on the end of his nose when he's concentrating on the paper or what horse to bet on. Dad was the eldest son in Nanna's family. Dad has to be one of the most inquisitive people I know. He loves to do crosswords and will complete them in quicker than record time. I'm sure if he went on 'Who Wants to be a Millionairre' he would walk away with the big prize, he would find it insulting if he didn't know the answers! The annoying part about this is that of there was a debate going on in the family be would most certainly always be right, he loved it but it did used to frustrate us and boy would he rub it in with us! He was actually the only child Nanna had from her first marriage to Bampie Barnett; he was killed during the war when my dad was only one. He was only 25 at the time but he was so unbelievably handsome. The strange and yet somewhat quite fascinating part about this is the fact that my Bampie Barnett, Bernard was his name too came from a long line of very gifted 'Spiritual' people who originated from Finland where they were all Reindeer Farmers. Go figure huh? Not only did we inherit the gift from Nanna's family, Bampie's are witches too! Listening to my dad, the gift the Barnett

The Seventh Son of the Seventh Son

family had was very rare but strong form of Telepathy. They didn't have phones in those days and relied purely on this form of communication. I wish I knew that years ago, I would have most certainly tried to work with it let me tell you! When Bampie was killed, his sisters and mum; our great grandmother and aunts still kept in close contact with my Nanna and my dad; after all, he was now related through blood and was the only grandson at the time so he was ruined. They were both very important to them and still are to this day. All the sisters would argue about who was going to have dad for the day. From what we know, Auntie Haze is the one to watch and learn from with the Barnett Gift.

The interesting fact is that all of the Barnett brothers and sisters had so much respect for my dad growing up. I guess they made so much of a fuss over him and that still hasn't changed even to this day. His nickname is 'The Don'! Whenever we have family gatherings as soon as we would walk through the door they would all bow down to my dad and start teasing him as if 'The Big Cheese' was here at last! Auntie Kath, Vilma, Barbara, Hazel and Uncle Tony absolutely doted on us all and would always make us feel so very special to them. All the Barnett's were very creative when it came to costumes and putting on a show. The all had their special talents and my goodness, did we have some fun watching the shows they would put on for family celebrations, whether it would be someone's wedding, birthday or engagement. They always went above and beyond what any of us expected to see. One time they all wore the 'Emu Costumes', with the false legs hanging over the side of the costume and then another time they wore 'Trash Men' costumes where they had the bins attached to their back and false people tucked inside them, it was just amazing, the attention to detail was just out of this world and at the time looking back on things, I'm sure they could have done something to include that in their show as musicians. All of

KICK START THE BROOMSTICK

Auntie Barbara's boys was in a band that they had created together. Auntie Kath was a very well known Fashion Designer 'Kath McVey'! I remember winning Rose Queen at the Cwmbwrla Carnival in Swansea when I was 10, she actually made my dress, cloak and Tiara, I looked like a Princess. I still remember the smell of her house today. The dress was the most beautiful peach color I've ever seen in my life and the material she used was raw silk, the dress used to stand up on its own on the floor, but I can just remember how pretty I felt on that day and it was all down to her! She was so talented but never really took her gift further for some unknown reason?

Now getting back to Uncle Fester or the wrinklies, as I like to call mum and dad. My dad's spiritual gifts are very unique indeed. As a child growing up in my Nanna's house he used to see the spirits come and go, Auntie Margaret in particular, that was Nanna's sister. She would often make an appearance in the bedroom at night. All of dad's brothers and sister would sleep in Nanna's bed whilst Bampie was away with work. She would place the side table up against the bedroom door to stop anyone from ever entering into it and would pace back and forth in front of the window, pull back the net and see if anyone was lingering around. If anything ever happened they would never have been able to get out of the door. Eventually she would climb into bed and that was where they would stay until the next day. Listening to his stories today, his experiences almost mirror mine as a child growing up. He was ten when he first saw Auntie Margaret but the older he got the worse things got for him. Everywhere he went all he could hear was the voices of the spirits trying to talk to him; only he didn't like it, it scared him. He wasn't sure if they were trying to warn him of things so being unable to decipher the messages he chose not to listen at all and sent them packing. Of course he did speak to Nanna about it but she never forced her beliefs on anyone, she knew Dad would come around to the idea one day. When he was a child in school, all of his friends used to ask him to read their palms and no matter what he told them it would always come true. I guess he used to learn a lot from Nanna, she always had people to the house to have readings done on a regular basis and so he would hide behind the door and listen. His predictions for himself were generally quite accurate also, I wish this was the case with me; I am wonderful at looking into someone else's life but absolutely rubbish at my own! One thing I can say is that Dad always followed his gut instincts on things. Dad would also have very strong premonitions, so much so that if he dreamt about someone he would absolutely dread seeing that person for fear that what he had seen would actually come true. The majority of the time it would. Going back then, Dad would also possess the gift that Allison does today, if someone upset him all he would need to do is put the 'Natural GYP' on someone and lo and behold, by hook or by crook it would happen. This kind of gift is actually more powerful than any of us that use cards because the results are pretty much immediate. I remember a man that used to socialize in Dad's local club causing my dad difficulty for quite some time. The man was just jealous of how popular my dad was and tried to force people against him if you will. This man did not expect what happened next; within weeks of causing problems for my dad he experienced a heart attack! I know you are probably thinking that's not fair, well we can't help how powerful we are with our gift and some things are taken out of our hands to prevent us from hurting that person further. Who knows, if he hadn't have had a heart attack and survived, he might have experienced more 'GYP' and died? This wasn't something we like to use but if we couldn't sort it out naturally then the Gyp would always come into play.

As a child a spirit who looked almost like a Wizard if you will often visited Dad. Who ever this man was he wore a long black cloak that almost glistened as he moved around the room but always stood higher off the ground as if he was on stage. This man/person/thing would always reassure my dad as soon as he appeared by saying 'please do not be scared, I'm not here to harm you, I'm here to guide you' only dad still doesn't know to this day who he was, what he was meant to be guiding him with or was he simply there to protect him from the vast array of spirits that would try and talk to him? The only one spirit that was truly allowed to show herself to him was Auntie Margaret and that was because it was Nanna's sister. What Nanna still to this day wouldn't believe is that her daughter Kathleen, who I was also named after was actually still born but used to show herself to people as a little girl tugging on Nanna's skirt whilst she would be in the kitchen cooking. Daddy was 21 one when Nanna lost the baby going back in 1965, she would have been around the same age as my sister Donna now, its such a shame really isn't it. My mum used to see her all the time and I too feel a presence of a female that I am not familiar with on a regular basis.

Another very unique but more intense part of my dad's gift is that during his sleep he will speak fluently in a completely different language. My dad is convinced he has had many different lives and I will have to say that I agree with him. The first time this happened it woke mum up and completely freaked her out in bed as he was talking fluent Chinese to himself. Other languages he has spoken out loud in his sleep is Arabic and is convinced he was an Egyptian God at one stage in his life but the most significant time is whilst him and mum were away on vacation in Turkey. He woke mum up speaking 'Old Biblical Tongue' only he was having a full on conversation with someone, mum was looking around the room to see if there was anyone there but there wasn't, it was just her and dad. They both called me from a street phone in Turkey the very next day to see if I could look into his episode the night before? This one scared Dad as you can imagine and he found himself asking lots of questions afterwards. For sure I would love to be able to record what he was saying and get it translated. I actually bought him several books on regression for Christmas last year because I truly thought they would help him but he is yet to really sit down and study them. He strongly believes that he lived in America in 1924. I'm hoping one day a Regression Session can give us some insight into his dreams. Dad is more than 100% certain that he 'Astro-Travels' throughout the dream process also. His dreams are so vivid, he remembers the slightest most insignificant detail but seems to jump from one time frame to the other as they did in the TV show 'Quantum's Leap'. I personally do not know of any other living human being to experience such a thing but I'm sure once this comes out so will lots of other people from the woodwork! The research I have done shows that between 8-50% of the worlds population are believed to have experienced this with the first documented one dating back to 1747. Dad has always shown an interest in Science Fiction and has in the past been fascinated by UFO's and the 'secrets hidden' by the governments all over the world. Dad and I do seem to have a bond with these things though; he's not comfortable still to this day in telling people his premonitions; predictions etc; excluding me. He will always call me to tell me or to see if I can research things for him.

Although it has to be said, our very own mum is somewhat of a witch herself, she always knew with us kids when if we were dating someone whether they were right for us or not! Both my sisters dated men called Paul at the same time believe it or not and she knew that they both wouldn't last. I was believe it or not engaged to someone once and she knew from the first moment she met him that he wasn't for me, of course at the time you think it's just her being her but she was spot on the money with all of them, she would just get an overwhelming sense of feeling in her tummy that told her when she was right or not?

Perfect Timing. Let's go onto the 2nd Generation Nanna Barnett, AKA, Cyncie and Nannie Noo (and Bampie Too)…

CHAPTER 3

Nanna Barnett the 2nd, to us at least!

It's funny actually, we still giggle each time we hear one of the kids call mum Nanna Barnett. Our memories of the 'very old' Nanna Barnett; our great grandmother are so very different to whom my mum is today. Actually she's a young and trendy Nanna most of the time. She's 5.3" tall, taller than my dad ha! Mum has mousy brown hair, not a grey hair on her head yet and still has beautiful skin. Mum also gained lots of other names along the way, 'Cyncie' being one, I'm not really sure who created that name but I know it was one of my cousins on the Forester side. All of mum's sisters had additional names that were shorter than their original ones such as Jenna for Jennifer, Eio for Eileen and Popo for Pauline. Nannie Noo was given to her from Ben, Donna's eldest boy I think? The standing joke though was Nannie Noo and Bampie Too! That had to be one of Donna's creations; she would always come up with the funniest things for the kids to say. She would re-write all of the classic songs into something ridiculous but they loved it, especially Charlotte when she was a baby. Charlotte is Allison's eldest by the way and the eldest grandchild also. Wait until you hear about her gift, it will blow your mind but not yet, you have to wait sorry. All of us kids have been through so much in our lives, which you will learn throughout. I think the only reason we have managed to cope is it's all purely down to mum. She brought us up with the mentality of 'tough times don't last, tough people do'. As much as we hate it each time one us are faced with life's challenges mum would always remind us of the fact 'what's meant for you, you will have'. She always inspired us to do and be whatever we wanted. All of us girls were ever so close to our mum I guess that's because she was so young having us all that she actually grew up with us if that makes sense yet she was still so young at heart? We always went to her with our problems and she would try her best to be non judgmental but sometimes couldn't help it, she would tell you like it was please or offend; however what you decided in the end she would support without a doubt. Everyone loves my mum; anyone you speak to has nothing but amazing things to say about her. She never got involved in other peoples business. Don't get me wrong, she loves gossip, giving and receiving it but won't ever get involved, she used to always say we had enough going on in our family we didn't need to be involved in anyone else's dirty laundry.

Mum and dad always struggled financially when we were kids growing up but it never stopped them from giving us what we wanted. Mum always worked more than one job, she would make sure we got off to school and she would be off to her first one, then by lunchtime she would be at her 2nd and then would be back home by 3pm to make sure we had our evening meal and then would be back off to work again in the evening to her last one of the day. Looking back now I honestly don't know how she did it, brought up four 'gorgeous' kids at the same time even if I do say so myself. I only have the dog and find that hard enough? Mum always had a great relationship with Nanna O'Conner; they used to go to Bingo together quite often. I still remember mum telling me now that Nanna made her wear lipstick and rouge the day she got married to my dad, how embarrassing is that? You see, mum never needed to wear make-up, she only ever used baby lotion on her skin and it shows today, she really doesn't have that many wrinkles at all but of course we are biased, she is very beautiful to us inside and out. For years after my Nanna died you could smell her in mums kitchen, and you would be sat in the dining area and all of a sudden these strange shadows and lights would show up on mums kitchen cabinets, they almost took the form of a person and we were convinced it was Nanna joining us! She used to love dancing after a few Blue Moons, that was her favorite cocktail? Almost like Irish Dancing and would sing the same song that no-one had ever heard of before 'A diddly ditey ditey ho, a diddly ditey do', and for years after we didn't understand what it meant until I purchased some old War CD's that actually played this song; I couldn't believe it?

It has been a very difficult road for mum as it seems to have been one thing after another and I know most people wouldn't believe what I'm about to tell you but every bit of it is true! It started out by Allison falling pregnant when she was 19, a long story which will follow when we get to her but mum decided to give up work and look after Charlotte so that Allison could finish her degree as a 'Qualified Chef'. Charlotte and Allison lived with us for the first four years but mum did everything for her. Charlotte absolutely idolized her and still does to this day. It was tough on her being a grandmother at 37, good grief, I still haven't had any kids and I'm 39 this year, can you imagine it? She had the four of us kids by the time she was 21 believe it or not.

I would not be sitting here in the position I'm in if it wasn't for my parents. When I first got the job on Cruise Ships I didn't realize the outgoing expense it took just to get you on board? You needed formal gowns, uniforms, spending money etc. Well the truth be known I didn't have anything in the bank at all but my parents recognized the opportunity it would give me so mum being mum took me to town and bought me absolutely everything I needed to go and even came to London and took me to a fabulous store called 'Sterling Bros' and bought me two amazing velvet dresses. I will never forget them although I couldn't fit into them for very long as I gained so much weight on my first ship. I never took it for granted what she did for me and therefore I always tried to re-pay them by paying for their flights to Miami or something like that. I wasn't the only one she helped; she also decorated both Terry and Donna's first flat that they moved into from top to bottom; she always tried to give us the best possible start in life; I guess this was because she would never have the opportunities we did?

Over the years mum has experienced things in such a short amount of time that some people don't even experience in their lifetime; one of which not even she expected. January 8th 2008 mum was diagnosed with Breast Cancer. Unfortunately she chose to have a Mastectomy due to the severity of the cancer growth. This was an extremely trying time on the whole family. I was still in America at the time when I heard the news. Mum text me to say that the results from the tests were not good and so I called her immediately. I could hear in her voice how scared she was. Now we all know how god works in mysterious ways and all I could think of was I had just taken vacation over the Christmas and New Year period; how could I possibly request more time off? Well, guess who got fired from their job three days later? Believe it or not I did but we'll save that hurricane for when it's my turn to talk but it did allow me to travel home for the surgery and I arrived the day she was due to go in. I just remember walking through the door in my parents that morning seeing this scared, nervous woman sitting on the chair. That wasn't my mum? I was so scared, we all were, my sisters had been amazing up until now, they took care of everything and truly tried to be there for my dad also. People forget about what the men go through during such a tragic time. I actually bought him a book written by a Cancer survivors husband to try and give his take on what a man can expect to feel and experience throughout the process of chemo and or radiation. Not sure he ever read it though? The day she came out of surgery was extremely tough on us all. Dad was there at the hospital first and as she started to come around from the Anesthesia she was all confused and in a lot of pain; it took every ounce of our being to be strong for her and Dad. You could see Dad filling up with tears but contained himself so not to worry her. It was a week or so until she came out of hospital and then once the tubes were removed from her scars it was time for Chemotherapy. The chemo following the surgery was probably the hardest of all. The girls used to send me texts crying when mums hair started to fall out and within days, she was completely bald. The only way I could make up for me not being there was to send her a few new headscarves home a week from Miami. I searched high and low for pretty ones, bandanas, what ever she wanted I sent her along with a 'Mothers Day Card'; I think I bought 30 around that special day because to us at this stage, every day was Mothers Day. Following the recovery, mum chose not to have reconstructive surgery. Her take on this decision was 'your father has been married to me for over 40 years, he's not going to love me any less with just one breast'. What a pretty powerful statement to make! Mum did however want to help the younger generation coming through having surgery but wasn't sure how and after many discussions with her cancer nurse we found out that there was a piece of machinery that could be used to transfer fatty deposits from the body into the breast directly after the surgery to remove the cancer; which would allow any woman to wake up cancer free yet still feel like a woman during recovery with the breast in tact. The hospital that treated her did not have the machinery in question and could not afford to buy one? One night during mum's recovery we decided to hold an annual charity event called 'The Cynthia Barnett Think Pink Foundation' to see if we could help raise money to purchase this machine; however the cost of it increased year after year and we honestly thought our goal was out of reach until Donna stepped in. She approached the Welsh Assembly to see if they could actually assist us; which in the end they did assist in placing one there on loan. We on the other hand continued to raise money and handed over a check to the Surgeon and Cancer Nurse in July 2010 of 15,000 pounds. We were ever so proud of what we had managed to accomplish; even the Lord Mayor of Swansea was there with his wife! The question we all ask ourselves at times is 'why is it that with all of these powerful gifts surrounding us we have never been able to use them to our own advantage? Perhaps to possibly guide us or warn us of a passing in the family even? This is extremely frustrating for us and has been especially hard on my mum. Not only did she lose our wonderful Nanna Forester, she lost Bampie O'Conner all within a space of three weeks. Of course this was just the beginning of the losses. Nobody on this planet would have expected what was about to happen or who was to go next. This time it was Allison's turn to pick up the pieces now.

CHAPTER 4

Allison Kelly, aka Sassan

Oh my, I don't even know where to start with this one. Let me just first start by saying Allison has always been the prettiest one out of us all, she always had the best teeth, unlike me and Donna who had to have braces growing up. Allison is 5'4" tall, blonde hair and always wears it in a bob style. She has always struggled with her weight her entire life and yet no matter what she had on she always looks stunning. As a child Allison was always running home with her report card and straight into mum and dad's hands it would go with pride and us three would panic walking through the door for fear of being grounded due to poor grades. Dad always used her as an example of how we 'should be' performing in school. Easter always makes me think of her because when all of us would eat our eggs as soon as we received them, Allison would save hers and then sell them to us weeks later! She was always wise with money. She would lend money to people but they would have to pay her interest back on top of the original amount. My dad used to tease her and say that moths would fly out of her purse if she opened it! We just nicknamed her the 'Miser'.

Allison fell in love when she was very young to a person at the time we all thought was lovely. One of the Paul's, say no more. They did everything together; he was a local boy and lived literally around the corner. Unexpectedly she fell pregnant at nineteen. Donna and I were probably the first to know prior to her telling my parents but after a very severe heartbreak Paul chose not to stick by Allison through the pregnancy; she was absolutely devastated but extremely worried about how she would be able to cope with a baby on her own. I think we all were at the time, we never expected to see this side of Paul at all, and he always came across as being absolutely in-love with her. His family was very strange though; his mum in particular was completely away with the fairies 'Cuckoo'! The best way to describe her is very 'Step ford Wife'. My parents gave Allison choices yet stood by her decision to keep the baby and provided nothing but immense love and support for that amazing little package that arrived into the world by the name of Charlotte Pauline Barnett. Charlotte brought so much love into the family you wouldn't believe. Being the baby of the family at the time I had my nose well and truly knocked out of joint and I have to admit, I was jealous to begin with but would love to spend time with her and sometimes babysit. Charlotte developed one of the most loving and contagious personalities you could ever meet. Not only was she funny, cute and loving she was fearless and unbelievably intelligent for her age. I guess being surrounded by adults she picked up on things so quickly. Charlotte was absolutely crazy about her mum and there wasn't one person on this planet allowed to say a bad word about her, she would yell and tell them off if she heard anyone try and say anything! So unbelievably cute! It was hard for us to see Allison so lonely; she truly did love Paul and was absolutely devastated. We used to share a bedroom and she would cry throughout the night, I never let on that I could hear her at all because as soon as morning would come, that brave face would be on for the world to see and she would be off.

Now of course, money was a concern for Allison and so she felt as if she needed some spiritual guidance. All of us were prone to experience a Psychic Reading somewhere along the way but Allison had a lady called Eirwyn that she visited quite often. Eirwyn had given Allison some pretty strong predictions regarding her financial situation, what she could expect to see in the future and told her she could expect to come into a large amount of money, not small but substantial and then on the night of July 1st 1987 whilst heavily pregnant with Charlotte she decided to go to Bingo with my mum. They were late and didn't think they would have made it. My Nanna and Auntie Irene passed them in a car on the way and they couldn't quite believe they never asked them if they wanted a lift even? Anyway, mum had been having these premonitions that money was coming from somewhere but couldn't understand where from and that night she was right, Allison shouted Bingo on number 72 during the U.K's National Bingo Game. They had just won Forty two thousand, five hundred pounds! How bloody fantastic was that! They called my dad in shock and he drove straight there. Afterwards they went to the Club to celebrate and Allison also won One Hundred Pounds on the slot machine! So you see, god steps in just when we least expect it. This truly did put Allison in a position that she could plan for her and Charlotte's future in a way she had never dreamed possible. They went on vacation to Australia to visit mum's sister Eio and her family and bought a new car also. It was so great to see her being taken care of and didn't need a man's help!

It took Allison quite some time before she decided to date again. It wasn't easy back then for someone to welcome a child into a relationship and she feared for years that nobody would ever love her or want to love her because she had a child by someone else. Don't get me wrong, she dated, sometimes I think for the sake of it but no one that actually blew her mind or swept her off her feet and she wasn't willing to settle for anything other than her Knight in Shining Armor even if he was delayed like mine! Instead, she decided to put all of her attention into her career and was an extremely successful Chef. Her cooking is simply amazing and I'm not just saying it because she's my sister. I've never seen anyone work that kitchen by herself in the way she does. You just hear 'MOVE' and you simply either get out the way or have the look of death from her. Her career went from strength to strength and by this time she was working in Unigate, the local distributor of fresh milk to the Wales and surrounding areas as the Head of Catering. This is where she used to chat to a certain special someone by the name of Simon Kelly. Simon and Allison used to sit and have coffee and breakfast practically every morning. Simon was not the type of person I think Allison would normally go for; he was quiet, pretty shy but very well educated and spoke so eloquently. He was quite tall and had a moustache, and thinning hair that he shaved off in the end, no smiling at that one please but let me tell you that I have never in my entire life met such a wonderful person. He absolutely adored Allison and spent as much time as he could with her. The amazing thing about this was he adored Charlotte also and knew that they both came pretty much as a package and didn't want it any other way.

Not long after they started dating Simon moved into my parents home with them. I was living abroad somewhere and my parents owned a holiday home in a caravan park that they stayed at to allow them to be together. You see, it wasn't just Allison and Simon in the house it was Donna and Shaun and Terry and Shivonne. You'll learn all about Donna soon enough. Allison fell pregnant; as did Donna on Ben and so did Shivonne on Lauren, so here you are the 'Power of Three Kids'. I think Allison and Simon were trying at the time to have a child but I would have to confirm that. Samantha Kelly was born quite poorly unfortunately and after several tests it was determined that she would have to undergo Open Heart Surgery at only nine months old. This put a lot of pressure on both Allison and Simon, you see Simon's Dad died at the age of Forty Three. There was always a fear that this condition could be genetic but Sammy Snail was such a tough little cookie that she pulled through. Her condition was called Tetra logy of Fallows; which means five problems in the heart and lungs. Sammy's surgery was difficult and the recovery was a slow process. They had to be so very careful when handling her the fun thing about this though is they nicknamed her scar the 'Zip' because that's where they opened her up on her chest. Allison and Simon didn't want her to be scared or embarrassed with the scar so to make it fun they called it the zip.

This family condition was always a fear of Simons and then not many years later, one morning Simon got up for work and told Allison that he didn't feel so good but proceeded to go anyway. Allison had told him to stay home but he didn't listen, he was pretty stubborn like that and didn't believe in taking the day off work for illness. Simon was sent home that day later in the afternoon as his superiors could see changes in his facial features and his natural reaction to things had slowed down dramatically. Simon only went to the doctors for a check up because Allison made him and after a thorough check up it would appear that he had experienced a stroke throughout the night that had affected him quite badly. His face had dropped on one side; which is a clear indication that stroke had occurred. His mobility on one side was very apparent and his speech had most certainly been affected, he was almost struggling to get his words out to start but they were quite muffled if you will. Now, of course this came as a shock to Allison and the family; everyone was extremely worried about him, especially his mum Avril due to the fact she lost her husband close to Simon's age. As a result of the stroke Simon was subjected to lots of different tests at the hospital; which determined the inevitable, he would have to have a Triple Bi-Pass Heart Surgery. I just remember receiving the phone call from my parents stating Simon was going into hospital and asking me to pray to the spirits to protect him. It was times like these that I wished I lived closer to home to be there for Allison and the girls. Simon's recovery was slow and painful, yet he did manage to impress the surgeons by how well he was healing. He was off work for almost eight months I think. Finally he decided to go back to work. He was only back in work one day on his normal job and then on the 16th of January 2006 the most devastating thing happened. Simon collapsed in work and was rushed to Hospital.

Allison was called immediately and frantically reached the hospital, only to find it was too late. Simon didn't recover from the massive heart attack he'd had and had sadly passed away. I remember this day like no other in my life. I was in work in Miami and my dad called me to tell me of the devastating news. I was stood outside the elevator in work when my dad called. I still don't know to this day how I managed to get in my car and make it home to call the family. The company I worked for at the time was actually fantastic with me; they allowed me to take a few personal days to gather myself and supported the fact I needed to fly back to Wales for the funeral. How do you pack for a trip to a funeral when the last time you packed to go home was that person's wedding? There's something seriously wrong with this picture. Somebody gave me a pill to take to calm me, as I just couldn't stop hyperventilating.

I was absolutely distraught at the thought of Allison having to bring the two children up on her own again. I think the best word to sum up my emotions at the time was ANGRY. I was so unbelievably ANGRY that after everything she'd been through she finally found the love of her life, a man that loved her unconditionally was now no longer to be

Allison Kelly, aka Sassan

a part of her life in the physical sense of the word. They had only been married a little under two years. Simon nagged Allison to marry him for years; however she always told him no due to the fact she was embarrassed by her weight and always thought she would never look good in a wedding dress. His last proposal was actually quite lovely; he tied the most beautiful diamond ring to a plant and gave it to her as a gift? She took one look at the plant and thought 'what is he giving me a plant for' and he had to prompt her to look closely at the plant and there she finally saw the engagement ring and accepted. The funny thing is, it was a standing joke at the time that Allison would turn up at the registry office in a trouser suit. Well, you will be pleased to know she didn't, she plucked up the courage and purchased the most stunning dress and cowl I think I have ever seen. Allison being Allison, a perfectionist to say the least had the whole day planned even down to the dressing of the room where the celebration took place afterwards. I actually went with her to help that morning. They were due to get married at 3.15pm if my memory serves me correctly, only we didn't leave the set up until 1pm! Allison even cooked and prepared her very own Buffet for the reception, and laid it all out spectacularly! This I have to say was partly because she knew she could do it better than anyone else around at the time and she wanted to enjoy the food herself. She had every hors d'ouevre you could possibly imagine and then some. The variety was probably over the top but that's just Allison, not only does it have to be perfect it has to be bigger and better than anyone else could do! I just remember us both running home to get ready; Allison even did her own hair and make-up the morning of the wedding. I wish you could have seen Simon's face as she walked down the isle; it was most certainly a Kodak and Master Card moment, absolutely priceless. He just couldn't believe how beautiful she looked.

KICK START THE BROOMSTICK

Both Charlotte and Sammy were bridesmaids and looked so pretty also. The photos taken on the day were so captivating; of course I took the winning shot of the confetti falling in front of them that I think everyone including the world and his wife had copies of. They had such an amazing day; the whole family loved it and I remember going back to Allison's house in the evening after the wedding and singing songs with the rest of the family until early hours of the morning. How is it possible that a family can go from such elation to such devastation in such a short period of time?

The day I walked into their house after just flying in from Miami for the funeral I will remember for the rest of my life. I don't even remember to this day who picked me up from the airport I just remember as we approached the house I felt as if I wanted to physically throw up. I became hot, shaky and with the unmistakable lump in my throat that I was about to vomit. I got out of the car and walked up the stairs to the house. I opened the front door and to the right hand side of the hallway was the door to the living room. I looked in and all I could see was Allison sat there on the chair at the side of the fire and she just had this upside down frown that I will never ever be able to forget. She was sat there not looking at anyone or anything; just simply lost with a pain in her heart that would leave an empty space for the remainder of her years. I could not stop physically shaking, I tried to be strong for her but seeing her made me simply fall to pieces. Allison was more worried about me shaking than her own emotions, I think I was hyper ventilating uncontrollably at one stage, we just both hugged each other and cried?

The next few days were probably the hardest few days I had ever had to deal with in my life at the time, I can honestly say that as a family once again we were each others rock. Charlotte and Sammy will tell you that they lost a whole year with their mum after Simon died. Allison completely changed, she was in almost a trance and lived every day on what has to be said was 'Auto Pilot'. Even she could not tell you anything about that missing year; she has absolutely no memory of it what so ever. Today Allison still misses Simon so very much and there's not a day goes by without her crying still. When she's sad she will go sit in the memorial garden she created for him at the back of the house to give her a little bit of comfort at least. I just remember getting back to Miami thinking I needed therapy? I seriously didn't know how to grieve? I'd never experienced a loss before, especially of this magnitude anyway. I didn't want to talk to anyone about it, not even my friends. I think I turned into a bit of a recluse at the time.

Now, being middle witch, Allison's gift is that of the 'Natural Gut Instinct' the GYP that you heard me speak of earlier and has an extreme sense of a person's nature immediately upon meeting them. Allison can walk in a room and know instantly if there is someone or something negative around her. In life we all have people who are either ultimately jealous of you or simply just don't like you and can't bare you to be happy or succeed. Allison cannot only spot these people a mile off she has had a few spooky experiences just like my dad where she put the 'GYP' on people. There was a man around her in work. Lets call him stupid for security's sake. Stupid tried very hard to get people to work against Allison, always gave her the worst shifts to work and said some pretty mean things to her with regards to her competency of the job. Now, you can say what the hell you like about us Barnett's but one thing is for sure, if we do a job we do with 150% effort and won't stop until it's done. For a while Allison let his comments bottle up inside her; which made us all very nervous. We all knew that when that happens the consequences of the thoughts inside her manifest into such severe backlash on the person who caused her to feel this way. Unfortunately stupid was in the direct firing line of this and it wasn't long until he actually fell ill and had to stop working. How did she do it? Imagine in your head the worst experiences you've ever had in your life all happening at the same time, imagine someone hurting you or a family member in a way that is just not imaginable. Now, imagine what you would do that person if you could get away with it? Take that force, sprinkle a little magic, and add the power of three and away you go! Deed done! Right or wrong, it's only Karma coming back to him. You see; no matter what people think about us, we are extremely protected by spirits to ensure our gift isn't wasted. Sometimes what we put out there takes a little longer to take manifest but we don't doubt the fact it will so all I can say is if you have done wrong by us in any way at all, keep looking over your shoulder, we are lurking in the shadows, we are sitting on the bottom of your bed, we are in your car, your home, your workplace, we are everywhere! Let's just put it this way, I wouldn't like to be one of our enemies!

After Simon died Allison started experiencing the strangest things take place around the house. Simon's nickname for Allison was 'Sas'. He used to say 'Sas get off your ass and make me a cup of tea'! It was so funny at the time because there wasn't anything bossy about Simon but he would be laughing saying it to her because he knew that if he didn't she would think he was being serious and would get pissed off at the way he'd spoken to her. Allison and Simon's home used to be a Manse, a home where the Vicar lived and the original stained glass is still above the front door to this day. Allison had decided to get the flooring in the hallway changed to real wood panels; it truly did look quite lovely as you entered. One night Allison was walking from the kitchen to the living room in the direction of the front door and she could not believe her eyes. The reflection from the stained glass windows on her new floor spelled out the letters SAS. Allison screamed, we all ran out to see what she was talking about and instantly we all had goose bumps the size of golf balls and was in awe of the fact that she had to have a new floor put in to see that or was it due to the fact she was never meant to see it before he passed away? This was just the beginning of the signs for her. I read for Allison not long after Simon passed away and he came through to me. He spoke to me about the front garden and how they'd take it in turns to go into the pub next door for a pint and then sit on the bench or the windowsill in the Summer time. He also spoke of a flower plant only Allison would understand; he had apparently bought her a rose plant one year that she has now placed in his garden at the back. It was really difficult for me to try and bring him through though; he could feel how distraught Allison was and tried to pull back during the reading, yet could not let go. I could feel his pain also. It's the first time I have actually been able to feel it during anyone's reading so this was a first for me.

Allison was a bit; ok a lot of a neat freak! She always knew when something was out of place and would pretty much have a go at who ever did leave things out of place. Now, on her day off she will spend the whole day blitzing the house from top to bottom and on this one particular day she was just finishing upstairs and had taken the vacuum cleaner back downstairs. As she walked into her bedroom she saw a crumpled piece of paper on the floor; thinking to herself that wasn't there when I walked out of here two minutes ago? She picked up the piece of paper and sat on the edge of the bed as she unraveled it. To her surprise and amazement it was the receipt for her engagement ring off Simon, she'd never seen this paper before and had no idea how much the ring cost etc. That wasn't the point here though, the point was how did it get on the floor and where did it come from? That was Simon showing her he was around again. She sat on the edge of their bed and sobbed her heart out; she missed him so much in her life. Another fantastic story was Simon had bought her a very beautiful gold bangle, only she had snapped it and could not find the other half anywhere. She thought perhaps she'd lost it outside the house otherwise it would have shown up at some point to either her, Charlotte or Sam. Then on Valentines Day a few years later, Allison woke up after crying herself to sleep thinking he wouldn't be around for another special day sat up in bed and looked at the dressing table as something caught her eye? Yes, believe it or not it was the missing half of the bracelet but it was also lined up with the piece she already had. She shouted to the girls to see if one of them had done this and they swore on her life they hadn't and then she realized once again, divine intervention had stepped in and allowed Simon to show Allison on this special day for love that no matter where he is, she will always be his one true love. God, I cry every time I think about that story. I just think to myself 'One day, that will be me, I will find someone that will love me that much he would do anything for me in life and in death'! We'll get to me soon, I promise. The theme on Allison and Simon's wedding day was hearts, they had them absolutely everywhere and now to this day after years of cleaning, when she's at her most lowest emotionally; you can guarantee from absolutely no-where either pink, red or silver hearts will appear just to let her know he's always with her no matter what.

My brother Terry played a very big part in helping Allison after Simon died. Terry and Simon were actually very good mates. They always tried to do things on weekends with the kids and were just generally really good friends. Terry and Simon used to have such a laugh together. After Simon passed away Sammy used to spend a lot of time up Terry's with Kelly and the kids, so much so that they even bought an extra set of bunk beds so that she could have her own bed. He tried so hard to make sure she didn't lose out on not having a dad around to love her and both he and Kelly treated Sam as if she was one of their own kids. He used to take her camping down the Gower Peninsula in Swansea almost every time they went as a family. Sammy loved spending time with Terry and the kids, she thought he was nuts! Some people did at the time think she spent more time up there with Terry than she did with her own mother but I guess looking back on it now; the frame of mind Allison was in at the time it was probably best she was there. That being said; anything Allison needed he would be there for her, whether it be to fix things around the house or just to talk to even? Terry and Kelly decided to name Becky after Allison. Kelly also missed having Simon around because he helped to keep Terry on the straight and narrow. He was such a positive influence for my brother yet always kept a close eye on him with his personal demons.

Well all I can say is once again perfect timing Miss Barnett; we can slip into the next chapter to tell the world all about your big brother Terry and his life.

CHAPTER 5

My Big Brother Terry, aka Professor Morris

O.K, you're going need the Kleenex for this part for sure! My brother was such an interesting character growing up. He has to be one of the youngest Entrepreneur's I have ever met in my life! Always looking for the next 'get rich quick' scheme! By the age of 10 he was well on his way with three different bank accounts that held his cash from separate ventures he was involved in, all from his own hard work though. One was his pop round. My dad at the time worked for a soda pop company and my brother would buy it at cost price and re-sell it. He even built his own wheel trolley to cart it all on. Another one was his paper round and the other was pocket money. He had these huge ideas of one day owning his own business and never really stopped until he was in his late teens. Terry was always bullied as a child in school due to his weight and pretty much never really bothered with anyone, he only ever hung out with the kids from our street. As he got older he did manage to drop his weight and was actually quite a hotty! He was 5'9" tall, blonde hair, blue eyes and a great cheeky smile. He always had the best clothes on and would practically buy himself something new every week out of one his cash funds. Terry was very close to the boys in the street, Shonty, Hamers, Carl, Mossy and Ian. They went everywhere together, they even had their very own 'Wolf' whistle that only they knew what it was, and it would be their very own way of finding each other. One person would whistle and the other would whistle back to let them know where they were. As the gang got older there would always at some point in the week be a fight with the Penlan boys! You'd always see them either running after or away from them but they never actually did get in serious trouble, apart from the time when one of them hit my brother with a Machete knife and nearly cut his finger off. He spent a lot of time in hospital having surgery to save it but I don't think the person who did it actually meant too? They would always threaten to beat each other up but it never really progressed into anything violent until this time.

I always used to hang out with Terry and the boys because there were very few girls of my age in my street so I didn't really have a choice. I was always the 'cling-on' that drove my brother nuts. I was such a tomboy at one stage. I used to follow him everywhere. He hated it in the beginning but him and I were such good mates that he always protected me. He'd act all tough in front of the boys but then when we got home he would always say sorry to me for being such a jerk! As a career he decided to go into car mechanics to start but ended up finding his forte as a Panel Beater, someone that sprays cars to perfection, well he did anyway. None of us were surprised at this because as a child he gained the name 'Professor Morris' from me and my sisters because every gift he ever had he always had to take it apart to find out how it was created then he would put the thing back together again prior to my parents even realizing what he'd done! He hardly ever went out to town drinking with his mates; he was always working on something. Normally they would hang out in the lane behind our house, they never really were into drinking to be fair to them, they all loved their cars too much and spent so much money on dressing them up it was scary. On his eighteenth birthday he met Shivonne Lee, she turned up at his party my parents had arranged in the garden for him and his friends with a single red rose. My mum thought at the time she was a pretty little thing, little did she know that devastation was lurking in her shadows. Terry seemed to spend most of his time with her once they started dating and used to sneak her into his bedroom at night thinking my parents didn't know. In the beginning she was a lovely girl, very pretty but not very well educated due to the fact she didn't really have a very strong upbringing. Her family, well most of them, were drug addicts unfortunately. Her mum was a nice enough lady but never strong enough to try and help any of them and gave up trying after a certain point and she unfortunately had to bring herself up from a young age. It was sad for my parents to watch seen as they had always provided is with such a secure strong upbringing.

Not long after meeting Shiv Terry started smoking and drinking and partying. My parents and the girls liked her as a person but could see what she was doing to him. It was almost as if he changed overnight. My mum found out that Shiv was taking drugs and really wanted to support my brother in trying to help her because you could see how much he adored her but my mum knew what was coming. She started to see such drastic changes in Terry's behavior and warned my dad that he was going down the wrong track. My brother was my dads blue eyed boy and he couldn't bare the thought of him taking the wrong track and didn't want to believe it until he saw it for himself. Over the next few year's things went from bad to worse. Shivonne continued to take drugs and Terry got involved with dealing them. To this day we still cannot believe this happened. Shivonne had given birth to Lauren at this stage and they were both taking drugs around her. When she was just a tiny baby my parents had come back from the caravan to check up on everyone living in the house and Terry showed up with Shivonne and

My Big Brother Terry, aka Professor Morris

the baby. He was so completely off his head on drugs that he started to have a go at my dad and said some pretty horrendous things that I refuse to repeat on here for pure embarrassment. My poor dad was just simply heart broken that day. He could not believe his boy had spoken to him in the way he did. Us girls and mum all cried at the time; we were all just so upset to see my brother in that way, especially me as I've always been away and was not exposed to this kind of thing. My parents always updated me on the phone but to see it for my own two eyes was astonishing. My mum used to ask me to call him and to try and talk sense into him, even though I am the baby he did listen to me. Although when it came to Shiv he never listened to anyone, he absolutely idolized her. I just felt so sorry for my parents; they didn't deserve this; it was hard trying to convince mum it wasn't her fault but I still think she feels as if she failed with him somewhere along the way.

Terry and Shiv fought like cat and dog all the time. She was so mean to him and treated him so badly, she used to physically abuse him when she was completely off her head and yet when she was straight you couldn't have wished to meet a nicer person. When she was 'Off It' she turned in a psychotic lunatic and would stab him with nail files and burn him with cigarettes? How could she possibly do that to my brother? After many years of arguing, two children later they split up. Shiv moved out and one day got arrested whilst the kids were in her care and ended up choosing drugs over her children and family. Terry fought and won full legal custody of the children because she was caught shop lifting in town, shocking I know but she did actually used to take the babies with her! Terry was very lucky at the time; he had my parents and my sisters as a support to help him with the children. I was living with him for a little while but decided to go back on ships. He adored those kids, I just remember feeling so sorry for him at the time

39

because no matter what Shiv had done, deep down he still loved her. The things he told me that she'd said and called him; not that it's an excuse but no wonder he felt worthless. It truly broke my heart.

December 2007 my brother had a huge scare. You see, he turned from drugs to drinking, only he didn't just drink socially, he drank to escape from the world all day every day. How Kelly put up with his behavior I'll never know, she must have truly loved him that's all I can say. He was taken into hospital with stomach pains and the Doctors warned him that if he ever had another drink again it would kill him. We all thought this would have been the scare that he needed; it was but unfortunately not for very long. One thing I didn't realize or even understand is that Alcoholism is actually a disease? I used to think people thought that was a cop out of owning up to the fact they had a drink problem but the stories I've heard about Terry most certainly has opened my eyes to a completely different understanding of the word 'Alcoholic'. I guess I just wasn't educated on what it was exactly and what the symptoms and devastating effects it has on the surrounding people who love you. He had the most beautiful children ever and I'm not just saying it because they're in our family, they were all so cute and funny with it. Kelly his girlfriend was so good for him, she didn't drink, smoke or anything come to think of it. I'm sure she had her own friends but she never seemed to bother with them, they were always together and they always did things as a family, Terry was such a fantastic dad. His only problem was his addictions. Research shows that if you're addicted to one thing you are prone to lots of other addictions? Looking back now, I guess you could see the patterns of his addictive personality. I lost count how many times mum would call me and say he would be off his face on something and cause so many problems in the family for us all, especially my parents. They were always there trying to pick up the pieces for him; more so from a financial standpoint because by now he was receiving legal fines that they would try and help him pay for, they did it for Kelly and the kids, not for him really.

The day my mum was coming round from her anesthetic after her Mastectomy, Terry walked into the hospital as high as a kite! It wasn't Alcohol because we couldn't smell it; it must have been pills of some sort. I just remember my mums face; she was so upset, so much so my dad asked him to leave the hospital. I felt so sorry for Kelly. She was so embarrassed bless her and really didn't know which way to turn. I've always been away so was never privy to that kind of behavior but I wasn't impressed and I made it very clear to my brother the next time we spoke.

The heart wrenching part about this was he couldn't help it. He'd been to rehab so many times. It would work for a little while and then he'd hide it from us all again. I know people say you have to want to change but I'm not sure he even knew how too? I think the best rehab he ever went through was when my mum and dad kept him with them until he came clean one time. That was all triggered from a terrible accident that was caused at his flat. Jeremy one of his friends was so high on drugs he thought he could fly and jumped from a five-story building and broke both his legs in the process. My parents walked into Terry's flat and it was full of Junkies laid everywhere. My mum screamed on the top of her voice, gave them all fifteen minutes to exit the property, packed a bag of things belonging to my brother and took him home with her. Mum stayed up all night and all day playing computer games with him, trying to do anything she could to save her son from this drug infested life he was living.

My parents used to take him everywhere with them, even to their local club as they were scared to leave him at home on his own for fear of what he might take. This did work at the time even though it has to be said it was very difficult for my mum to see him go through the natural Detox as he did but he did recover, only once again, not for very long. This when the dealing came into it. Terry was heavily involved in big cash dealing and managed to keep it all under control for a while but then managed to get himself into so much trouble over it. This was the only time I think he was clean. It truly felt like if it wasn't one thing it was another with him. One of the things I need to clear up is the common myth that 'It must have been his upbringing? Well let me put the record straight, it wasn't the case this time. He had no different treatment than the girls and myself. The issue here purely lies with getting mixed up with the wrong crowd. We thought meeting Kelly would have helped him and it did but there was only so much she could do also. Christmas Day 2008 my parents called everyone from my apartment in Miami to wish them a Merry Christmas and to talk to the children and my brother told my parents he and Kelly had decided to get engaged. They were absolutely delighted and thought this could have been the turning point for him. Let's plan his wedding and his alcohol free future.

For months after he came out of hospital he continued to drink, he would hide it from everyone except Kelly who knew instantly as soon as she looked at him whether or not he'd been drinking. His best mate Steve told us he would drink the bottle of Vodka down in one go and then within minutes throw it all back up, I guess it was the feeling inside as it ran through his veins that used to be the satisfying part. I hate throwing up at the best of times, I can't imagine doing it purposely but again, like I said earlier, it's a disease! Everyone kept asking him to stop for the children's sake, by now he had six in total, two with Shiv,

My Big Brother Terry, aka Professor Morris

Kelly had Travis by a previous relationship and then they had three together. Kelly begged him but he just seemed to go from bad to worse though unfortunately then on the eleventh of March 2009 he told Kelly he wasn't feeling too good and so he took a bath to see if it would help his tummy but he had a very restless night sleep. The next morning he couldn't get out of bed and Kelly called the Ambulance. Terry was rushed into surgery immediately. They identified internal bleeding but could not find where it was coming from but his stomach kept filling up with blood. Unfortunately he never regained consciousness again. Saturday 14th March around 12pm the unthinkable happened, my big brother passed away. I remember receiving the phone call from my mother telling me that I need to arrange to fly home and I was hysterical crying on the phone begging her to not let them turn the machines off until I arrived home but it was too late, he just wasn't strong enough to survive the surgery. All of his organs had collapsed and there was absolutely no way of him ever recovering from that and sadly, at that very moment he left us. I know what you're all probably thinking, how selfish of him to just think about himself when he had all those beautiful children to take care of? Yes, we all thought those thoughts and were extremely angry with him for not listening but it wasn't for the lack of trying. I don't think any of us really truly understood what a dark place he actually was in. I guess we, me in particular hoped he would grow out of it.

How do we ever begin to pick up the pieces after yet another tragic death in the family? Terry was only thirty-eight years of age! How will Kelly ever be able to handle the children on her own? Will she want to keep Lauren and Daniel with her, after all she didn't have too; they weren't her kids? How will my parents ever come to terms with burying their son? This is wrong; you're not supposed to bury your children.

KICK START THE BROOMSTICK

You're supposed to go first? Not in this case unfortunately. How were they ever going to heal from this? The Thursday night he was taken into hospital is the night I personally think he left his body because it wasn't long after the girls called me to let me know he'd been taken in that I went to bed. During my sleep I was woken up by him sitting on the side of my bed. Now, bearing in mind he was a lump of a boy so I could feel the dip in by mattress. All he did was wrap his arms around me, gave me the biggest hug and told me he loved me and then I woke up in absolute hysterics of tears. I sobbed uncontrollably and could not stop. Poor Sooty. My little puppy was licking my tears away as they were rolling down my face. I remember texting my boss to let him know that I'd be flying home that night and then it was time to pack. I remember sitting on the chair upstairs in my apartment thinking my life is about to change, yet I wasn't 100% sure how. I don't have any idea how I got to the airport, I don't even remember leaving Miami? My body had simply become numb to my surroundings. What would I face when I got home? What would be the outcome of all of this? I took some sleeping pills as soon as I got on the plane and then Charlotte and her girlfriend Pat picked me up at Heathrow. I knew that as soon I stepped back into Swansea, my life would change forever, in more ways than one which you'll learn later on. I just didn't know what to expect the day I walked into Kelly's house. I think I was just scared to see the children; I wasn't sure of how they were going to be and as soon as I saw Kelly's face I just burst into tears. The funeral preparation was even more difficult for us to handle than any of us expected. We were all sat around his kitchen table with strange looks on our faces and one minute we would be in tears and then the next we would be in fits of laughter. We knew one thing, we didn't want the Vicar to speak on behalf of us, my brother wouldn't have wanted that so we decided as sisters we would put a Eulogy together so that everyone there could truly understand the person he truly was; not the person hiding behind the drink and drugs.

This is the Eulogy to our brother Terry:

Our brother Terry had many talents as a young child and many names to go along with it. As far back as we can remember we knew he'd end up becoming the 'Best Mechanic' around. Ever since he was a young child, he dissected every mechanical Toy he ever had with immense curiosity. He had to know how they worked and put them back together again perfectly before Mam and Dad ever found out. Therefore very appropriately he earned the title from me, Donna and Allison 'Professor Morris – The Teabag Inventor'. One Christmas, he almost blew himself and the house up trying to fix the Tree Lights before Mammy came home. Yes, it worked, the Tree Lights lit up and so did my brother. He twinkled like the Star he was then and will always be now (he electrocuted himself basically, just as well he was sat on the sofa because he would have been fried burning his hands in the process!).

Arthur Daley was the second nickname we gave him. Terry would sell Sand to the Arabs and Ice to the Eskimo's and make them think they had such an absolute bargain. So much so that by the age of 18, he had 3 bank accounts. He was always on the search for his next 'BIG CHALLENGE'.

Water Baby was the next name we gave him; whether we were in Looe and Polpero in Cornwall or Greenways in Oxwich, come rain or shine, thunder or lightening, we always knew where he would be…turning blue in the pool. Nothing fazed him; he had the courage of a Lion and the strength of an Ox.

KICK START THE BROOMSTICK

Being the only boy, we all allowed him to get away with absolute murder. He would get Allison to chauffeur him to work every day; Donna would iron all his clothes for him to 'Dress to Kill' with his Gel and highlights in his hair and I would be the 'Keeper of his Secrets'; and trust me when I say; there were quite a few. We always knew when Terry was home from work; the kitchen always smelled of Swaurfeger and his bedroom window would be wide open with UB40, REM and Bob Marley blasting down Torrington Road. You could hear him sing, or try too but it was very painful; he didn't care, he loved it and that's all that mattered.

What many of you here today don't know is that for two years Terry was a single Dad to Lauren and Daniel; something he absolutely cherished until he met the lady that changed his life. She brought life into his veins and love into his heart. Kelly was Terry's saviour; she always kept him in line; he knew how far he could go with her. Together, they built such an amazing life and produced the most beautiful children, Lauren, Daniel, Travis, Shannon, Becky and Demi, whom they both adored with every breath that they took. Kelly, thank you for being the best thing that ever happened to our family. We gained a sister the day Terry met you and I can speak on behalf of our parents and the girls, we love you very, very much. Thank you for loving him the way you do and making him the happiest, most proud man in the world.

Our Dad used to drive a 'Big Tipper Lorry' when we were all small and he would always sit Terry on his lap and pretend that he could drive. Terry loved it and always wanted to drive his own when he grew up; which he went on to do only 3 times as big. He was our parent's Blue Eyed Boy; they only ever wanted the best for him and were so extremely proud of the person he turned out to be.

My Big Brother Terry, aka Professor Morris

We all were; never more so than when he turned up to Donna's 40th Birthday party as Dafydd Thomas 'The Only Gay in the Village'. He absolutely loved it and couldn't wait to dress up again. On his way home he and Kelly decided to stop at Eaton Road Fish and Chip Shop. When the lady behind the counter asked 'Salt and Vinegar on your chips', Terry said 'Is that Gay Salt and Vinegar Myvanwy'? The whole chip shop was in hysterics laughing. That was our boy's sense of humour.

The last note we want to share with you all today are the first words our mother sang to him when he came into the world and when he left the world in Mammy's arms:

'He's my little boy, my baby boy
He is my darling my pride and my joy
Two big blue eyes as blue as the sky
He's Mammy's little boy…'

CHAPTER 6

Donna Wonna Turner

O.K, now it's time for the 'Big Cheese'! I think everyone on the planet knows not to mess with my big sister Donna Wonna. My brother and his kids started to call her that when they were babies but then the name has stuck with us all for years. We still use our nicknames today, mine is Pangie by the way, Angie Pangie! A bit like Bond, only NOT ha ha! All through school Donna was known as being a bit of a tough nut to crack, nobody messed with her. Allison was quite lucky actually because there was only an 11 month age gap between them so they were very close and have always hung out as friends as well as being sisters. Allison was in the year below Donna in school and always had her to fight her battles if need be. They had both left school by the time I got to senior school and I remember the first day I met the Principal Mrs. Price, she said 'If your like Allison you can stay but if your like Donna you can go' ha! I was petrified of her from that moment on and nobody would have ever lived up to the expectations of Allison anyway, she was such a SWOT! That means always studied hard and ensured she got the best grades, only it also means you're a bit of a geek! I am a geek only of a different kind, which you will learn.

We always looked up to Donna being the eldest. When us girls were younger we shared the bedroom and she used to sing us to sleep at night time or she would let us listen to Radio Luxemburg until we

Donna Wonna Turner

fell asleep. My parents would allow us to sing for a little while but if it went on too long mum would shout through the wall and tell us time to sleep. I remember that bedroom vividly; Duran Duran and Queen pictures all over the wall. Donna was convinced she was going to marry John Taylor. Three single beds used to fit in that room and three wardrobes. Of course being the baby my bed was always next to the radiator. For years we had blue flowered wallpaper, blue curtains, blue windowsill, white ceiling and bluey grey carpet. It wasn't until Donna moved out that my parents decorated it for us again. We had the Black and White TV on the dresser in between the wardrobes that we used to take it in turns of watching between us girls and Terry; one night we would have it and the next he would. Donna and Allison used to pay me to tidy their mess up and clear the beds by the time they came in from town; I would love it, they'd always spoil me! If ever they brought supper home they would wake me to see if I wanted any and you could guarantee when I woke up the next morning I would find garden peas scattered across the bedroom floor that came out of one of their hand bags.

Being one of the most popular kids in school at the time, Donna was never short of boyfriends; someone was always asking her out. Only the very few made it home to meet us but on one condition, they had to be special, that and they fact they'd buy me sweets so that I wouldn't tell my parents they'd been in the house when she was supposed to be baby sitting for me. Donna was very select in who she chose to spend her time with and if you look at her today, most of her close friends from back then are actually still around today. One in particular, Louise Macarinelli. Louise and Donna go back as far as I can remember as a child. They were always together. The funny thing is; Louise is a twin and Jayne her twin used to hang out with Allison, how odd is that? Anyway; Louise came from a very strong Italian background so her rules and regulations from her dad were pretty much the same as ours; don't pass the deadline of the time you need to be in otherwise you'll be grounded. Her and Donna were little buggers growing up though. Always into something? Lou had many sleepovers at ours and that was the only time I would be allowed to be privy into the conversation but they made me pinky swear on the 'Sister Oath' that I would never repeat what I'd heard. Good god, can you imagine betraying their trust and have to face the wrath of Donna? No thanks, I still have dirt under my belt today but will carry it to the grave with me now.

Donna couldn't wait to move out of the house and live on her own. It was such a tight squeeze for us; especially as they are women now really and wanted privacy. That and the fact she didn't really see eye to eye with my dad; he was extremely strict and liked to shout a lot. Come to think of it he still does? Donna told my mum that she was looking but could not afford to do it on her own so once again mum came to the rescue and helped decorate one of her very first flats that she lived in. I remember the best flat she had was when she lived with the 3 Karen's in the Sandfield's in Swansea near the City. Donna would call me on the day she'd been supermarket shopping and invite me down to raid her goody cupboards, I used to love it! They used to have so much fun together and were all very close. The flat at the time was pretty trendy; I think it was four or five bedrooms; living room; tiny kitchen if I remember but was split-level. Now, it was during this time that she met back up with an Ex-Boyfriend, one that I absolutely detested by the name of Paul 'Ike Wife Beating' Turner. There was always something that bothered me about him. At the time I couldn't for the life of me tell you what it was, I just knew I had the most horrible feelings in my belly whenever I was around him. He was a spoilt brat from the Mumbles in Swansea, which was quite a wealthy area. If he wanted anything he would just go running to his mum or his Nan and they would give him whatever he wanted. He always had the best of everything but If I came home with a new pair of boots or anything that was in fashion at the time (I was again, a little bit of a Tom Boy), he would have to go and buy them first thing on the Monday morning, he was pathetic like that! Putting my feelings aside Donna loved him more than anything else on the planet at the time and eventually married him after being with him 14 years?

They tried desperately to have children but unfortunately Paul was unable to produce. This was extremely frustrating and upsetting for Donna, she just couldn't understand it. I remember everyone giving them tips on how to conceive and they must have tried every old wives tale in the book but to no avail. Looking back this was probably God's way of saying 'you deserve more'? You see Paul used to physically abuse Donna only she hid this from the world and the family for the longest time. He used to beat several different colors out of her, that and whilst she would be working nights he used to pick up other women and take them home and sleep with them in her bed? Now I hope you can understand why he'd make my skin crawl can't you? I just absolutely knew deep down in my heart he was bad news, I just wish I would have been able to warn her at the time but I was too young to truly understand my gift back then. Paul was also very controlling and would only allow Donna to go to Bingo with my mum. He thought that would be the only place she wouldn't meet someone new? Well, God works in mysterious ways and if the Universe wants to throw you a bone he will. Donna's came by the name of Shaun Homewood, the Bingo Caller! Go figure? Donna secretly became friends with Shaun and then eventually decided to leave Paul and the horrible life she'd been subjected too for years. My mum prayed and prayed at the time that she would never have had kids with him, I know that sounds horrible but if you met him you'd understand why? I think deep down as much as my dad wanted her to have a child he also knew she wasn't for him. Within months of Donna and Shaun being together she actually fell pregnant on Ben then a few years later on Ashleigh Poppet so it just goes to show that what's meant for you, you will have. It was touch and go when she had Ben though. We nearly lost both of them; she had a terrible birth and Ben was born with Bells Palsy, the collapse of the facial muscles due to the stress he experienced at birth. Even as Ben grew older, when he was tired you would still see the signs in his face of what he had been through. Today you could just simply eat him, he's so unbelievably cute and will break a few hearts one day I'm sure. He was 16 July 2010!

Donna is such a doting mum; she will absolutely go without for herself before her kids do. They have everything and then some. She struggles each year what to get them for Christmas because they have everything they could possibly ever want! They always do things as a family; which is great and I truly admire that with them. When Shaun has the night off work Donna won't even pickup the phone to you unless it's an emergency because that is their time and she won't let anything or anyone get in the way. They love their vacations together and try to go somewhere every year but their favorite has to be Florida. They've been lots of times but a few years back they came out to Orlando and so I drove up from Miami to spend a few days with them. We had such an amazing time. We visited the theme parks, the restaurants etc. One night we decided to stay and hang out by the pool at their hotel and have a few drinks. What happened the next tonight was history in the making for Donna; this was the night her spooky side rose to the surface and her spiritual gift came to light.

I remember this night clearly. There we were sat there chatting and all of sudden Donna started hearing a woman speak things to her? I honestly did think it was weird to start with; only because she hadn't done anything like this before. We sat there for hours whilst I wrote down what she was saying and then one voice led onto another and before you knew it, we'd been sat there for almost 4 hours. Lots of beer and wine later, we both fell asleep on the bed and woke up with quite a large hangover to say the least! The next day I'd scheduled for her to have a full Spa day for her birthday, she wanted a facial, massage, Manicure and pedicure. Whilst she was having her feet done the staff member introduced herself as one of the names the spirits had given her the night before. This kind of made her nervous then after asking several different questions it just so happens that the girl's brother came to Donna the night before and passed on several messages to her for the girl and her mum. The mum worked as a hairdresser in the same salon and was also there so there were lots of emotional tears as you can imagine and Donna just could not believe this was happening to her and all I remember saying to her was 'welcome to my world'! It did take Donna a while to come to terms with having her gift but before long she was on that broomstick and was off! I was so unbelievably excited because now I had someone who could understand what I had been going through all these years. Her gift just seemed to go from strength to strength after this experience and I have to say she truly did amaze me at how well she adjusted to it. I guess she was one of the main people I spoke too about my own experiences so I don't think it was that hard for her really. Over the next few years Donna tried all sorts of different ways to bring out her gift. I bought her the first pack of Tarot

KICK START THE BROOMSTICK

Cards but I think I bought some that were too intense for her to understand. They were quite gothic if I remember but I just thought it would be nice for her to try and bring her gift out the same way as I did but for some unknown reason she couldn't take to them. Every year I would come home on vacation from the US and would always bring some things for us to try and play with, whether it was Gypsy cards, Angel Cards, Voodoo Dolls, spells, all sorts of things but Donna took such a shine to the Gypsy cards she asked me to leave them with her to play with so I did. The reason I was drawn to the Gypsy cards in the first place is because of our national heritage being 'Romany Gypsies'. These cards were glued to Donna's hip and the more she played with them the stronger her gift became and now she was doing readings for all sorts of different family and friends. Donna was convinced the connection she had with these cards was meant to be; she was a little scared to be quite honest because as soon as she touched them she would feel something unbelievable; just as I did with my Tarot Cards? She couldn't quite understand where the magic came from but all she knew is that she almost had an electric shock as soon as she touched them. It was very powerful and quite overwhelming for her but she knew her gift was very, very strong and that she needed to nurture it carefully.

Something you need to know about Donna, not only did people 'just' start going to her for readings; they've always gone to her with their problems. She has always been a bit of an agony aunt to everyone. Even some of my friends that missed having me to talk to found themselves knocking on Donna's door for comfort and advice but most of all a hug! I used to call her all the time from the US and as soon as I would speak she would instantly know if I was O.K or if I was upset for some reason or another. All I would have to say is 'Hi Donna

Donna Wonna Turner

Wonna' and what ever she picked up on she would react too instantly. Now if I called and either the football or the rugby was on I would have to call her back ha! Nothing or no one, not even me would have the power to take her away from the box! As a person, Donna is as straight as they come. Please or offend she will only say it like it is and yet she is one of the funniest people I know on the planet. I don't think she even realizes how witty she is at times but she is so quick with her one liner's and has to be one of the only woman I know that can use profanity and actually get away with it! My dad really doesn't respond well to that side of her; he absolutely detests women swearing at the best of times but you could still see him fighting back the smirk on his face trying his best not to laugh at her. My Nanna Forester was the best with Donna; they would wind each other up something rotten.

Donna has always been career oriented. She's worked for Social Services for almost 20 years now as a care worker with adults with special needs. Donna is so fantastic at what she does because of her caring nature. She started out working with people that were considered 'border line'; which means they are not 100% mentally stable but do have a lot of normal tendencies about them. Then she showed a great interest in adults with challenging behavior and for the next few gruel some years she was battered and bit to pieces by some of the service users but would come home every day so phenomenally excited and could not wait to get back the next day. Over the years Donna progressed in her career and took on more of a senior role. She worked very hard and was willing to do whatever was required of her to climb the ladder. Unfortunately, Donna created some enemies along the way that were basically jealous of not only how good at her job she was but how well she got on with the other staff members and service users. Donna being Donna will never as some people call it kiss ass and therefore unfortunately she was held back in reaching her goals due to this. As frustrating as this was for her she was also very hurt because some of her work colleagues that she thought were friends turned out to be the complete opposite and actually went behind her back to ensure she didn't get the promotions she wanted. It took Donna a long time to come to terms with the betrayal but for years I had done her readings and it clearly showed success was coming only as we keep saying unfortunately, which you will learn later on that there is no timing in the spirit world so when messages come to us as much as we can try and give what we like to call a 'guestimate' sometimes we can be wrong. The information we give is never wrong, it might take longer to come to fruition but it always does and that is again on a please or offend basis. After many years of trying for senior roles and being turned down, time after time, she never gave up and eventually she landed the perfect role! Today Donna is so very happy and it just goes to show that all good things come to those who wait.

Now let's talk about Ashleigh, Donna's baby girl. Ashleigh is Thirteen now but all through her life we knew she had the gift. She used to get up out of bed in the mornings and walk into the kitchen and give Donna messages from whatever spirit had visited her the night before. Whenever I would call Donna Ash would come on the phone and she was so spot on with the men I would be dating at the time. Pretty scary really seen as she was only about seven years of age when the first message came. The biggest thing that happened was when my mum was baby sitting for her one night. Mum was sat on the sofa and Ash was on the chair watching TV and she turned to mum and told her that Grandma was sitting at the side of her grandma being Nanna Forester, mum's mum. She told mum that Grandma hoped she got the flat she wanted? Mum was awe struck because she never told anyone about this little flat that she fancied, especially none of us? Ash proceeded to tell her that Grandma was O.K and that she misses her very much. My mum could not believe her ears; well she could knowing she was one of us but was so happy to hear that her very own mum was sat at the side of her on the sofa.

The perfect time to catch a girl and bring out her witch qualities is before they reach womanhood. When I found out that Ashleigh had the gift I did everything in my power to try and help bring it out. I sent lots of different books back from Miami to try and help her to understand what was going on. Donna gave her the Tarot I bought her but it was way too intense for her to understand. She did read the books I sent for a while but as she got older, as most teenagers did she put more attention on boys that she did with her gift. That was to no fault of anyone in particular I must say; Donna was busy with her life of not only growing her career but also managing a house with a partner and two children. I wish I would have been in the UK at the time to try and develop it further but hey, as we spoke of earlier timing is everything! At the moment Ashleigh is still searching for answers with her gift but has also shown a great interest in other religions; which Donna has tried to help her explore. It's amazing how things just happen at the right time for the right reason. Now Ashleigh isn't the only grandchild that has the gift. Terry's kid's do in a very intense way but we'll get to that later. Now it's time to talk about Charlotte the eldest grandchild and her, very unique and ever so amazing gift.

CHAPTER 7

Charlotte Barnett, aka Charlie Girl

O.K. Charlotte Barnett! This is an interesting part of the story. Charlotte has had to be such a tough cookie since she was a child. As much as she never missed out on anything up until Simon arrived in Allison's life she still used to ask questions about 'why don't I have a daddy'? It used to break Allison's heart but Charlotte did actually nickname one of my uncles daddy, it was cute really because she used to use his name following it. He really spoilt her as a little girl also. For some unknown reason my parents knew from a very young age that Charlotte would grow up to possess the gift. Especially following what happened next. Their thoughts were confirmed. They were both taking photos of Charlotte in the living room, it must have been some kind of special occasion or she had a new fluffy dress on or something like that anyway and the TV was actually turned off in the background. A few weeks later mum went to collect the photos from being developed as it used to take almost three weeks in those days, not one-hour photography like today. As she started to sift through them she could see a reflection on one of them of someone in the TV. As she looked closer she dropped the photos with shock and asked my dad to look at them and tell her what he could see in the background? To mum's surprise dad confirmed that what he could see was Jesus Christ's face and reflection to the left hand side of Charlotte. My mum agreed and they both stood in the kitchen with the largest goose bumps on their arms you could possibly imagine. This whole experience just confirmed their original thoughts. Mum called Nanna immediately and asked her to call over to see the photo and as soon as Nan looked at it she said 'this child will always be protected by Angels'. Little did we know then that once again, those very words would be spot on! As you can imagine the family paid close attention to Charlotte following that incident but it wasn't until Charlotte was ten years old that she started to see and feel spirits around my mum's house. The first time this happened Nanna O'Conner actually touched Charlottes arm whilst she was stood in the kitchen and she could smell her perfume all over her. Every time she would enter mum's house she could feel Grandma close to her but would never be scared and soon as they all sat down to tea in the kitchen the shadow would appear back on the kitchen units and they would all say hello to her. That's what Charlotte used to call Nanna, Grandma. Charlotte started to have repetitive dreams all the time of a woman that told her she was her Guardian Angel called Edna? The woman came to her all the time but she knew there was nothing to be scared of, she used to wake up and feel nothing but peace in her heart but motivated to go about her day with a smile on her face. As you can imagine at such a young age Charlotte had questions about what she was experiencing but by now the family were so much more open to discussing it and they welcomed it and I think it triggered my dad to start talking more about his experiences with the family.

Charlotte's most amazing experience was when she first had a visit from the Angels. She was only eighteen at the time and Simon hadn't long passed away. To give you an idea of the kind of person she is she struggled immensely with trying to overcome Simon's passing. Charlotte absolutely adored him and to some degree she felt guilty that he had gone. Not long before his passing she had spent many months thinking about her real father and wondering if she should try and reach out to him, or find him at least? I guess like any normal child that had been through this similar situation wanted to know why he didn't want to love her or want her in his life? She suffered severe depression afterwards and would find herself crying to sleep on most nights. One night the tears had stopped, she was laid in her bed both mentally and physically exhausted. The lights were out and all she could hear and feel was things flying in front of her face; she felt the draft that followed them tickling her face almost and she thought for one second 'am I dreaming; do I dare to open my eyes?' only when she did she was absolutely amazed at what was she was seeing. Right there; before her very eyes were the tiniest fairies, Angels and Cherubs all flying, laughing and singing around her bedroom. Charlotte remembers the colors being so bright and electrifying it took her breath away. The Angels were of Regal Nature, very astute and in control of the situation but were no larger than the others. They wouldn't show their faces to her yet the Fairies were smiling, singing and jumping and bouncing all over the room where as the Cherubs let off most light but she could feel the connection with her heart. They had the cutest but modest smile of all. Charlotte didn't know what to do; she froze for a while but then realized they were there to help her and to put peace back into her heart that was missing since Simon's passing. The tears of emotion ran down her face but they weren't tears of sadness; they were tears of overwhelming joy to know that she truly was protected just as Grandma had told her years earlier. As you can imagine it took Charlotte a long time to eventually get to sleep but when she did she couldn't wait to go and tell Allison what had happened the next morning.

Charlotte Barnett, aka Charlie Girl

She sat on Sassan's bed and practically relayed the whole experience. Allison just held her in her arms so close to her heart and they both just had a very special moment; one that no-body will ever be able to take away from them. Allison wiped away Charlotte's tears, thanked the Angels and the Fairies for the experience they gave her and they went about their day. For the next few weeks Charlotte did find some solace in her experience and kept that moment in her heart yet life and it's ups and downs found her emotions on that roller coaster from day to day. Her bedroom was her only retreat. She found herself hiding behind that door to try and understand why life was being so hard on her family. She was angry; she was upset; she was sad yet was happy at the times she did have with Simon. It was 9pm on a random Tuesday night and she was once again laid on her bed thinking of Simon; still crying and then all of a sudden she felt as if her arm was dead. She turned around to see why her arm felt to so strange only to see her arm had levitated into the air and was held by an immense light that was almost too bright to see; she blinked and instantly it reduced in size and she could see Simon holding her hand and the love she felt could not be explained; only her heart could understand what he was trying to tell her. When the light disappeared she felt an inner strength like never before but came away from it with a message 'please be strong for your baby sister Sammy and my wonderful wife your mum, Sas'. Charlotte knew in that moment she needed to change and to take control and to help Allison come to terms with the new life they had ahead of them. This was yet another fantastic experience that she will never forget. Over the next few months Charlotte continued to have visitors in her bedroom only sometimes they wouldn't show themselves to her. She would be laid in bed and hear clothes sliding off the chair and of course her natural reaction would be to turn the light on and see what it was; what clothes fell? Only when she did nothing had changed; nothing had fallen? This frustrated her for a while. I think the biggest frustration has been the noise of the plastic bag rustling? Several nights in a row she would hear this noise however when she'd turn the lights on there was no bag in the bedroom and still to this day she doesn't understand this significance. Perhaps one day she will? Charlotte loved her bedroom. It was the only place she could express her emotions without upsetting Sassan and Sammy. Whenever she found herself sitting there thinking things would happen. The TV would go off and then come back on even though she was no-where near the remote controls. The lights would flicker and whenever she touched a switch on the wall she would get an electric shock that was visible to the human eye? Well, that was until Charlotte was in College and the tutor that was taking her class for the full term saw it for her own eyes on several occasions!

Charlotte struggled for years with her emotions and how to bring them out. She always wanted to follow me in my footsteps with my business success and when she was a child my parents had business cards made with No.1 Grandchild printed on them because she wanted to be just like me. She always looked up to me and thought if she followed in my footsteps then she could possibly be as successful. Charlotte decided to take on the Hairdressing course in Swansea and qualified with flying colors, pardon the pun yet it wasn't making her happy. I remember calling her from Miami telling her NOT to follow the hairdressing route; even though it made me the person I am today it was hard, extremely hard for me and I didn't want her to have to experience that hardship. I truly felt knowing her personality that she would be more gifted and suited to Beauty Therapy; more so Holistic Healing. I had visions of her doing Reiki and Acupuncture and had to

Charlotte Barnett, aka Charlie Girl

share my visions with her. Charlotte was feeling so low at the time it was difficult for me to try and inspire her; yet I wasn't willing to give up. After all I don't get sign's for no apparent reason, only with her they were very strong. The day I called her it just so happened that there was a family gathering taking place in Allison's home and it was brought to the surface that Charlotte's depression was bigger than anyone could have ever imagined; she shared with my sisters and my mum that she had thought about dying; possibly committing suicide she was that depressed. None of us had any idea that the sadness she held in her heart had developed into such tragic possibilities. I was on loud speaker explaining to her what I'd seen for her future and that she had to trust me; I'd never let her down before and that I'd seen her reaching success above what I'd ever done before?

Over the next few weeks Charlotte spent some quality time soul searching and believe it or not did decide to look into the Beauty Therapy course. She applied at the local University and was accepted! The family was so proud of her but something was still not right. She still had a secret that she kept from us all that still kept the tears in her heart. The secret she was hiding from us and the rest of the world was that she was actually Gay and had know she was different from probably the age of Ten. Apparently her first experience was when she was Fourteen yet she was still in school and was so embarrassed by it, she felt almost dirty and wanted to hide the emotional evidence as much as possible but as she got older she was actually living a lie. Between Simon's death and now this? Charlotte was on the verge of a nervous break down; she didn't want to be in this life of lies. When she was Nineteen years of age she met the most fantastic person called Pat. Pat was Twenty-One at the time and they actually worked together at Mecca Bingo Hall in the evenings. Charlotte has worked there for years to help herself get through University financially. They fell in love instantly and all of a sudden Charlotte completely felt at home in her heart; she knew this was the right path for her. After several months of dating she plucked up the courage to tell the family who she was and not hide her sexuality any more. She remembers the day very well. She asked Allison and mum to be there as she had something to tell them. Instantly they thought she was going to say 'I'm pregnant' because Donna had predicted that years prior. Instead, she came out with 'I'm Gay and I'm in love with a woman'. HOLY SHIT! Can you imagine the response?

Poor Charlotte, Allison reacted as she always does completely over the top and basically disowned her. She came out in the November I think it was and Allison didn't speak to her until the January. Allison is very old fashioned like that and couldn't honestly come to terms with it; she was absolutely devastated and mortified at what people would think. I think she thought as we all did that it was probably just a phase and that perhaps Pat had led Charlotte astray? The interesting thing here is that I read her cards for her the year before and I saw someone coming into her life. I described what I thought was 'HIS' qualities turned out to be 'HER' qualities. Absolutely everything, from the natural curly hair to the complete Geek that this person was going to be; this is Pat to a T! Her nickname is 'Pat.com' because she can pretty much do anything with regards to computers, IPods, phones, printers, you name it she can do it! We absolutely adore her. I remember the first day she met the family was the day I flew home to Wales for mum's Cancer surgery. Donna had invited the whole family around for Sunday Lunch and she invited Charlotte and Pat also. Bless Pat; it's hard meeting the In-Laws as it is never mind the whole family all at once. Suicide ha! Everyone welcomed her; she was very shy but then again no one will ever be able to get a word in edge ways with our family when we are all together and if anyone interrupts; especially if it's not family you will simply receive the look of death! We don't choose to be mean but I guess it's just a natural Barnett reaction.

The day mum had gone into hospital Allison had decided to have a girly night at hers for us all to catch up since my arrival home. Donna asked Allison if she was going to ask the girls to come and believe it or not she said yes! We could not believe what she was saying so Allison called Charlotte and invited them both there. That night I have to say we all fell in love with Pat.com because she won our hearts through her absolutely loving nature but more so through her hilarious sense of humor. She has to be one of the nicest people I know. Charlotte is such a different person since this happened. She's almost come alive? That's the best way I can put it. Pat not only loves her she provides her with the emotional support she needs and most certainly motivates her to succeed with her career. Charlotte has absolutely flourished in University and has been hand picked by the tutors themselves to apply for additional courses i.e. Reiki, Acupuncture etc. She has most certainly put my talents and experiences to shame. Charlotte is most certainly gifted with her hands and her healing. Allison converted the study at home into a Spa for her and she has managed to build herself quite large group of return clientele but as much as this has been wonderful she has much grandeur plans for her gift. Charlotte wants her own Spa and who can blame her really? She's spent all these years in University to build a successful career for her herself; you can't really blame her for not wanting to work for someone else. Unfortunately setting up your own business isn't easy and not cheap; this is where I come into it but before I proceed to tell you what happens next I think it's time to learn about me. After all, I'm just been rambling on to you all for the past hour or so and you still have no idea who I am? You'll get used to the rambling part soon enough; my dad used to say to me 'Angela, you don't give your gums a rest do you?'! And so here is my story.

CHAPTER 8

Angie Pangie, aka The Dumb Blonde

Oh my goodness that's all I can say. If you need to do anything, do it now before I start because once I do I probably won't stop until 2012! Let's start by saying I am the baby of the family and will honestly have to agree with the old saying that the youngest always get away with murder? I can agree because it's true. Growing up I was spoiled rotten not only by my parents but by my sisters also. You see, the family doctor originally thought I was deaf and dumb because I didn't speak until I was two years of age only they soon discovered that it was due to the fact my sisters and my brother used to speak for me; this was actually how I gained the title of 'The Dumb Blonde'. You'll realize I made up for this later in life as you read on but for now, enjoy the journey. As a child I was actually quiet according to my mum, I was never a bother and would always pretty much do my own thing; strange at times I guess but I always felt that I was never alone and I can say that for as far back as I can remember. I'd always pretend there was someone around me having a lovely chat with me whilst I'd be playing, only now I realize it wasn't imaginary for the most part? We'll come back to that later but so you can understand who I was as a child it's important for you to get to know me? I was always the one that would get the blame for things I didn't do by my sisters and my brother; well they tried to blame me but my parents would always see through what the others were trying to do. I hated disagreements. It would break my heart if I thought someone was upset or if I'd upset someone or if someone argued in the house I would always try and patch things up with them; especially my parents. Whenever they would fall out I would say 'daddy, hold mummy's hand and mummy, hold daddy's hand'? How cute was that? I just loved harmony around me. The slightest fear of stress or tension in the family I would break out in the most horrendous cold sores practically all over my face and to this day doctors don't quite understand why I get them so severely? The not so bad thing about this though is my skin heals so unbelievably well that I am left with no scars what so ever. I thank my parents for those fantastic genes. Don't get me wrong; we all suffered from cold sores even my parents but I would always look like Freddy Friggin Crougar every few months. When I didn't have cold sores I was a tiny cute little blonde thing! Always with different color ribbons in my hair, my mum always did special things for school with my hair. I remember sleeping with rags in my hair on more than one occasion so that I could wake up with ringlets or pretty little sausages they were called then.

That was a family favorite for weddings so god help if you were a bridesmaid because you'd sit there for hours in my Nanna Forester's house waiting for your turn and someone always ended up screaming 'They are to tight' but you'd get a slap on the legs, given a glass of pop and a biscuit and told to go sit in the parlor and basically zip it.com. My mum always had my hair clips and bobbles match whatever clothes she used to put on me bless her. It's funny really isn't it the stupid things you remember? All through school my mum always entered me into beauty competitions. I remember winning one; which I spoke of earlier, the Rose Queen but I think I did win some other trophies along the way but something had to give when I lost my two front teeth; not a good look let me tell you. I remember always wanting to be in the school plays and wanted to sing all the time. The first big role I landed was Little Red Riding Hood in Clwyd Junior School in Penlan, Swansea. I think was only six at the time because if my memory serves me correctly we were moving into our new home in Torrington Road around the corner from Nanna O'Conner and I think I still had my cloak on one day and it was snowing. I still remember the smell of that costume to that day and the amount of people that used to approach my mum when she would come to collect me was quite a surprise; you'd swear I was on Broadway, not in Penlan a small 'nowhere place on the map'! That school was awesome though, all of the teachers were ever so friendly and I think we all did relatively well from an educational stand point.

O.K so off to senior school I go and this cute little pretty little thing was no more. My teeth grew back and protruded out so that I almost looked like Dracula, honestly. Between I had too many in my mouth I had to be put under the Orthodontist review for braces I turned out to be a right stunner right? Wrong, I hated my life. I should have had a fixed in brace in my bottom teeth to straighten them but I refused to go and the only reason I got away with it was because my mum did the same years prior and guess who's teeth I had, yes same as hers! Now add that and a few pounds of what my parents called 'Puppy Fat' and I've turned into a right looker! I always thought I knew what I wanted to do when I left school and that was in the Performing Arts. I could never dance I have absolutely no coordination what so ever but I did adore going to drama class and singing in music class. I guess I always saw it as a bit of an escape where you could pretend to be anywhere in the world you wanted and to become anybody you wanted to be in the blink of an eye. I always was a bit of a dreamer. I'd find myself many times throughout the day wandering off to the land of 'anywhere but here'. I never really did take an interest in anything other than Music and Drama. Geography I was actually very good at; which did come in quite handy some years later on in my life, which you'll see soon. I guess there were other things I was pretty good at but didn't see the point in following but one that I loved was Dress and Design. Many occasions I would get into trouble for cutting up one of mum's bed sheets trying to create something fabulous to wear! I actually did have a knack even back then of doing things differently or trying to be at least anyway. I still like that side of me today and every now and again I will get creative and think 'O.K, what shall we make/paint/create today?' Only sometimes I do have to bring myself back to reality and remind myself 'Your not Martha Stewart'! Now my interest in drama and singing kind of got distracted by my very first boyfriend Mr. Dripping. We'll keep his name discreet but the select few family and friends know who he is. I met him when I was fourteen and dated him until I was Seventeen. I absolutely adored him but unfortunately as kids do, we grew up and grew apart. Funny thing is I've still kept friends with his mum all this time.

So what was a girl to do now? I had absolutely no idea of what I wanted to do in life. I was never inspired to become a Lawyer or an Accountant or Doctor? Those things were never options as far as I can remember anyway so I decided to follow my friends and go into Hairdressing. What was I thinking? I was accepted on a British Government course called the Hairdressing Training Associates course; which lasted for two years and had to find a placement in a Salon somewhere. I went on two job interviews at the time and was turned down but then landed the perfect role in a trendy little salon called 'The Cutting Rooms'. I worked for the two owners A and J and oh my goodness; they were completely nuts, just like French and Saunders! I had so much fun working there and stayed for three years, I truly did love it but once I received my certificate I was eligible for more money and they basically didn't want to give it to me so I moved to a Salon down the street called 'Mad Caps' and let me tell you, there wasn't one sane person that worked there including me? I was actually very nervous about going to work there because they all dressed completely outrageous and I was rather boring I'm afraid to say but it's not long before two of the girls took me under their wings and truly did look after me. I loved it there.

Now at this time I had found myself another boyfriend and again we will call him Derek because that is his name to me and I'm Muriel to him. OK people, try and stay with me, I promise to explain all soon. I dated Derek for probably a little over six months and fell hook line and sinker for him. I thought he was the best thing since sliced bread and would have done anything for him. Prior to dating him I had gone on several other dates but can't even remember their names; that goes to show you how much of an impact they made on me. As for Derek, I can't ever remember laughing the way I did when I was with him. He had the driest wittiest sense of humor. Going back in those days, we both lived with our parents and so it was difficult to have quality time together. We'd go out for a few drinks in a pub but that would be it. The highlight of our night would be when we played regular cards, playing cards I mean and I will go on record and say that he has to be the biggest cheat I think I have ever met in my life but I will say, we did also have such a giggle. He used to frustrate the pants off me but I adored him and therefore didn't really care. Derek, just so that you can paint a picture in your head was absolutely gorgeous. 6'3" tall, very athletic body and he had a bit of a dirty tinge to his skin color and so had the most distinctive look; perfect skin but it was his smile that won my heart. We met in a Bar in Swansea City called Central Park. I had actually been out drinking all day with my friends and we had decided to just stay out and not go home and get changed so were pretty drunk by the time he came into the bar. I just remember sitting at the bar with my friends looking over at him, thinking he had the most perfect peach shaped bottom that I'd ever seen in my life, I mean I think you could well of easily parked a glass on it. Anyway my friends dared me to pinch his bottom and of course after several drinks I had the Dutch courage to do it and I think it scared him more than shock him. Here was this pint size drunk blonde girl thinking it was hilarious stood in front of him laughing? It got his attention though. We spent the next few hours chatting. Apparently he already knew who I was through his friends. It was his birthday that night; he was twenty so we sat at the bar and celebrated for the next few hours. He was originally meant to go next door to a nightclub with his friends but chose to stay with me.

He asked to take me out on a date the next day and I accepted only I had had a little too much to drink and so couldn't remember whether he said he would call me at 4pm the next day or pick me up so I sat next to the phone dressed waiting for the phone to ring! I remember him pulling up in his sisters car outside; he didn't have his own at the time and I was shaking, this man made me so nervous and I didn't know why? Over the next few months we had a blast; we were inseparable and I wanted to spend as much time as I could with him, yet we both retained our own friends and did our own thing. He used to drive past the salon I worked in every day and would always look up with a kind of shy look on his face. Oh my goodness; my heart would skip a beat every time I saw him. I don't think I have ever had this kind of connection before with anyone else but I knew it was so much more than that, I had fallen in love with him and there was nothing I could do about it. I didn't want to fall for him initially because he told me up front that he was hoping to move away for a better career opportunity.

He had this tough guy persona to the world but to me he was so very gentle. We never argued, apart from the time we actually broke up. We'd only really ever laugh with each other; especially if I would stay over at his parents after we'd been out, his mum would tell him to go to bed and then he would sneak downstairs to be with me; we literally were like kids with our hands over our mouths to stop ourselves from laughing. Anyway, things started to get pretty strained between us due to the fact he was going to be leaving Swansea soon to move away with work; only no-body knew where he would be moving too. Then one day unfortunately we broke up just before Halloween in 1990, I found out he had gone for drinks with a friend of his who was also dating someone else and her friends tagged along with him? Even though to this day he promised me that nothing happened that night I guess the thought of him going out with other women was enough for me. I was heartbroken at the time and truly did think we would have patched things up because we still spoke. He still called me. He still picked me up from work to go and cut his hair and end up having tea at his house. We would be drawn to each other like magnets when we were out with friends of our own but all I could remember was thinking 'I can't stay here in Swansea with all these memories', how was I going to cope without him being around me? I knew that when he moved away he would probably meet someone else.

It was inevitable really; you see he had a high profile job in the Marketing Industry and had women flocking over him. I knew that the day he left home I wouldn't stand a chance of getting him back, I mean why would he choose me over a six foot model right? Truth is,

KICK START THE BROOMSTICK

I honestly didn't think I was good enough for him. I didn't look like the usual girlfriend of a high profiled person but I thought if I try and make something of myself as far as my career goes then I will stand out from the crowd, the models with legs up to their necks, the stick thin bodies and plastic boobs he would have to notice me then and so I did. I pretty much changed my destiny in that split second and sent off for an application to work on cruise ships. I never in my life thought I would land an interview but I did and I was ecstatic. My mum was wonderful to me at the time and she traveled up to London on the coach with me for moral support; I was so scared. We actually stayed overnight because there wasn't a train or coach early enough to get us there in time for the interview that morning. My mum was simply amazing, she would do anything for us and I knew in my heart that if I did get this job; as much as she would be delighted for me she would also be devastated at the thought of her baby moving away from home. I was 19 at the time and I remember sitting on the bus on the journey up to London feeling so stressed. I had a confession for mum. I confessed to her that I smoked cigarettes; I had to tell her because I was so nervous for the interview that there was absolutely no way on earth would I be able to go four hours without one. Back in those days you could smoke on public transportation. My mum reacted in the exact way I expected; she told me she was disappointed but I'm mature enough to make my own mind up but that she wished it were just a phase I was going through? Oh boy, we got off the bus in Victoria Station in London; we were both pretty scared; the only other time I'd been to London was for Hair Competitions at 'The Royal Albert Hall' only I was being driven so I didn't need to think of how or where I was going. We got to the tube station and made it to Euston Station where the interview was taking place the next day;

found a Bed and Breakfast and checked in for the night. I don't think I slept a wink all night.

So the dreaded morning arrived. I was so nervous but felt excited at the same time; my mum had bought me all new clothes, I looked quite lovely. When I reached the interview I realized that it was a group thing? Basically I was placed in a room of over 30 people and had to stand up and say why I thought I would be suitable for the job! I was crapping it let me tell you but somehow I did it and felt sick and dizzy the whole time! Don't even ask me what I said because I don't have a clue. I know I've lost ten minutes of my life somewhere but I do remember her telling me to stop and that I had said enough! I remember my nail snapped and was bleeding as I was sat there yet I was numb; I couldn't even feel the pain. This first part of the interview was to weed through the men from the boys if you will. I think the biggest thing they were looking for was confidence; I didn't lack that and made it through to the afternoon interviews where you had to show your creative skills as a Hairdresser.

My mum in the meantime was meant to be sitting in Euston Station in London having a cup of tea whilst she's waiting for me. She started chatting to one of the other candidates mums and they decided to take off on a little journey of their own and ended up in China Town! I was sent to a different location in London for the second part of my interview but I received a phone call whilst I was in the middle of my practical part of the interview to tell me she was lost and was in a major panic bless her! I had someone who worked in the store speak to her and give her directions on how to get back to where she needed to be. I was so embarrassed but worried more than anything. Some adventure this was turning out to be. I was sent out into the streets of London and told to approach two very random people and ask if they would model for me to do their hair? Are you nuts? People don't even look at you in London let alone speak to you? O.K, I plucked up the courage and was so lucky that I actually found an American girl called Mara Motley, she was wild and very loud but she accepted the challenge! I guess this was my first experience and a taster of what it was going to be like around an American person, after all that was where I was hoping to go if I had the job. I really wanted the job and thought I did relatively well with my practical; I even sold products to both my clients to help them take better care of their hair and apparently that was a good thing because the company I interviewed with were strict with retail sales and revenue targets! Being the person I am; I knew that if it were meant to be then I would get this job. I didn't want to keep my hopes up; there were so many people there interviewing; I really didn't know what kind of person they were targeting. After saving my mum we travelled back to Wales and spoke about the interview the whole way home. I was buzzing with excitement and thought even if I didn't get it well then it was a great experience.

A week went by and still no news then I received a call in work from my mum to say that the company had just called to say 'I GOT THE JOB'!!! Oh my god, I couldn't believe it, I was physically shaking with excitement and could burst! Mum told me I was leaving in two weeks time? Are you nuts, how can I leave in two weeks time? I had no money but of course I didn't think about that when I interviewed, that was just a tiny insignificant detail that I would deal with if I had too. My congratulations letter arrived in the post and it included a list of things I needed to take with me. I was so scared to tell mum because I didn't have the money to do it. When she read it all she said to me was 'If you want to go me and your father will pay for you'. I was over the moon and gave her the biggest hug on the planet. Now, there was one person I was not looking forward to telling, yes, you got it Derek! He'd called me in work that afternoon and we had arranged for me to go for tea that night. I remember feeling sick when I arrived at his house. He was in the bathroom window shouting out to me 'so, did you get it?' and when I said yes he almost smiled a sad smile but tried his best to be happy for me bless him. My heart was on the floor because now I realized I would not be around him anymore, was I doing the right thing? I don't know if I made the right choice or not, my Nanna seems to think I most certainly changed my destiny that day but I guess the truth of the matter was that I was running away from my feelings, running away from Derek. Don't get me wrong, I truly did want this opportunity to travel and see the world but if we hadn't of broken up or he wasn't moving away himself then I would have probably stayed here and like I said earlier; I needed to prove I was different; I needed to stand out from the crowd in order for him to see me. I needed to listen to the signs I was receiving from the spirits also; they had never let me down before.

So the clock was ticking and as the time drew nearer I was starting to panic somewhat. Everyone kept asking me if I thought I was doing the right thing and that it wasn't too late for me to change my mind if I wanted? My friends and family had all arranged to have a leaving do on the Saturday night which was so much fun. Then on the Sunday the whole family were at the house for my send off. I was still secretly hoping Derek would have called to see me but he couldn't face me; he didn't' do goodbyes in person but he did call me to wish me luck. I remember telling him I loved him before he hung up the phone and all he said was 'I know' and told me not to look back once I got on that train, only think about the great opportunities you have ahead of you. My parents took me to the train station after the family party and I remember being in shock, I'd never seen or heard my dad cry before. It has to be one of the most heart wrenching times of my life. We were sat on the bench in the station waiting for the train to come in. My mum slipped me one hundred pound and told me not to tell my dad and to be careful. The train approached the platform and they both hugged me and I got on the train. I was crying uncontrollably at the time and scared out of my mind; unsure of what was going to happen when I arrived in Earls Court in London. As I sat on the train I placed a tape into my Walkman that Derek had given me from his car and played it the whole way up there, hoping and praying I had done the right thing. All I could think of was I hope my grand master plan works out and that I hope it doesn't bite me in the butt. All I know is that if I weren't meant to leave I wouldn't have got the job would I?

CHAPTER 9

UP, UP AND AWAY

I think I pretty much cried for the first hour and with two suitcases in tow, what I didn't realize now was that I had to get them on the tube to my final destination? How the hell was I going to manage that and for those of you who don't know London at all, the people are not the most friendly in the world and would never think to ask if you needed any help. This was a huge problem for me and I have to say I was so scared but in a situation like this I think adrenaline just takes over. I did eventually make it to Earls Court so now all I need to do is find the address of where I was staying; can't be that difficult right? I asked a guy that worked in a Pizza Place if he knew where it was and he told me to just keep walking about ?'s of a mile up the road and I'll see it! Sure, two steps at a time with my luggage, stopping for a breather and then another two steps. By this time my hands are absolutely full of blisters; I'm freezing cold, as it's the beginning of December. I knocked on the door and was greeted by a Russian woman who beckoned me in. It was only then I realized it was a flat that I would be sharing with eight other people, all-foreign. I was the only British person in the room! Good grief; three Germans; three Italian; one French and me and they were all Gay. Even the women were Bi-Sexual! Please bare in mind I had never met a gay person up until this very point and didn't know how to be around them but I have to say they completely took me under their wings and looked after me the whole time I was there for about two weeks until I moved to a different flat around the corner because the company were getting rid of the one I was in due to cockroaches!

I was in London training for almost four weeks; which was hard. Every day we had to catch several different tubes back and forth. We only earned basic tips from working the floor and that wasn't every day because we all took it in turns but we managed. Eventually I was given my placement on a ship called 'The Tropicale'; which was Carnival Cruise Lines. I was also told that you were only allowed to take a certain amount of luggage with you so here comes mum to my rescue again bless her. She came all the way to London just to take back the things I wouldn't need and repacked my case again. I was kind of scared but not completely as two of the other girls that were in training with me at the time were also joining the same ship, phew, what a relief! So off to Puerto Rico we fly, up, up and away! I remember being in the cab from the airport pulling into the port thinking 'well that doesn't look like the brochure' it was so much smaller? We walked on board and were told we had fifteen minutes to get showered and changed into our uniforms because we were starting work immediately? Truth is I absolutely hated it in the beginning; the standard of hair we worked on was rubbish, it was all hair ups and shampoo and blow dry's. What a complete change from Mad Caps! It truly was a culture shock for me because my lifestyle and passion for my job had completely changed.

There were so many rules and regulations I felt completely trapped at times but after a few months I began to settle down. I started enjoying myself in the Ports of Call and loved the Caribbean with a passion. We were based out of San Juan in Puerto Rico and visited Venezuela; St Thomas in the Virgin Islands, St. Maarten, Grenada and Aruba. I was truly having a blast. I missed my family terribly though and would call home whenever I could. I missed Derek with all my heart and would write to him all the time. There was no such thing as Internet in those days; it was the good old-fashioned letter! He did try and write back on a few occasions bless him but his letters consisted of a hello, how are you and then would be packed with jokes from him! I would lie on my bottom bunk in my cabin and read them over and over and over again and shed more than a few tears in the process. They say you don't know what you've got until it's gone and I have to say I absolutely agree. I missed him more than words could ever express and I did tell him in his letters. Derek was never the kind of person to truly open up and share how he felt; which was frustrating at times but I always knew in my heart what he was thinking and feeling somehow. We just had a bond like that; each of us just knew by looking at each other and I knew he was missing me also and as much as I didn't need the words to tell me I knew in my heart. I was gone for Eight months with that contract; it felt like an eternity but I do have outstanding memories. I didn't think I would have done another contract though; I thought I would stay home, after all I'd done it now right? My parents came to pick me up from Heathrow Airport and they walked straight past me? They didn't recognize me; between I'd gained almost 14 lbs in weight and was orange with my sun tan they just didn't see me and I remember my dad saying 'oh my god you are orange' and mum saying in a polite way 'you look well', fat she meant but wouldn't upset me by saying so! Of course, there was a huge welcome home party for me once again at my parent's house.

My sister Donna had designed a banner with a cruise ship on it and they hung it outside the house. The whole family was there to welcome me home; it was lovely to see everyone. Later that evening my family and friends decided to go into the bars in town; I was hoping to see

KICK START THE BROOMSTICK

Derek but didn't unfortunately. I'd heard through the grapevine that he was scheduled to move away the very next day and so he called me that very next morning because he had heard from his friends that I was home. Just to hear his voice brought tears to my eyes and he asked me to call up his parents to see him before he left. I wasn't sure of what to expect and so here I am once again walking down the stairs of his parents. He's stood at the door waiting for me only he's wearing glasses and looked hot. Right there in that very second upon seeing him I fell hopelessly back in love with him.

We continued to see each other when he'd come home for the weekend from London, that's where he ended up relocating too with his job, but it was hard and then I got restless at home. I wasn't sure I would be able to settle after what I'd experienced and I was right, I got itchy feet. I wasn't seeing him as often as I liked and I could just sense that we were drifting apart. I wanted to go back away again, run again. I needed to think and so I did. This time I ended up on the Canberra, a very old British ship that sailed out of Southampton in England. It has to be said that this ship was absolutely fantastic; it was like working at home because ninety percent of the crew was British or from the UK somewhere. The crew even had it's own bar called 'The Pig'! What great laughs we had in there. This ship was the making of me from a travel perspective. I was only scheduled to stay for a few weeks but then something happened and the girl I was temporarily replacing decided she wasn't going to come back so I was offered to stay on board for the World Cruise. Oh my goodness; I couldn't believe it, I was going to travel the whole world and get paid for doing it all at the same time. I was absolutely delighted as you can imagine and after all I was still only 20; I guess someone was looking out for me up there. Now, the great thing about this ship sailing out of Southampton was that I got to see my family quite regularly; my mum and dad would come down the most and she would always bring my favorite food, Corned Beef and Branston Pickle Rolls and my Nanna Forester would make a huge ice-cream tub of Welsh Cakes for me; it was awesome. I loved having visitors; it made being away from home that little bit easier. I used to take them on a tour of the ship and then we would go into the town for Chinese. Homeports were always the best. We couldn't wait to get our visitors passes in.

Derek and I kept in contact on this ship also as there was a crew phone on board and I would try and call him from most home ports but then I left for the World Cruise and it was difficult for me to reach him. I sent him a postcard from every port and tried calling him from Hawaii, Sydney Australia, Japan, New Zealand, and Fiji yet he was never around to take my call? I knew something was wrong I could just feel it inside my stomach. I kept getting the upside down butterflies in my belly every time I thought about him and then we reached the very last Port of Call, Lisbon in Portugal, and I received a letter from him telling me he had decided to get married to someone else. I am filling up with tears as I'm typing this because I remember that day so very much as if it was yesterday. I thought I was going to die. The pain I felt in my heart was absolutely horrific; it took my breath away and I just remember trying to focus so that I didn't fall in front of the people in the crew mailroom. I was sitting in the Spa on the Ship and my boss was at the side of me; she was amazing to me about it and really made sure someone was with me the whole time. I just remember crying uncontrollably on the open deck thinking 'why?

Apparently I was right all along, he met a model and within three months of meeting her he married her, he was only Twenty-One! All of the team I worked with rallied around me; I think they were concerned that I would have I would have done something stupid. I can honestly say I have never felt so low in my entire life over this letter and in the end I had to burn it to stop torturing myself each and every time I read it. I just couldn't understand how someone would know if they were ready to spend the rest of their life with someone they barely even knew after such a short amount of time. The day he was supposed to get married I did a very scary thing; I sent him a Telegram, as there was no such thing as text or email in those days it was either Telex or Hand Delivered Telegram and I chose the latter. I begged him not to go through with it, maybe this was unfair of me but I had to try and do something; I knew this man was meant to be my soul mate not someone else's? I know he received it because his mum told me but it was to no avail unfortunately; he married her. As much as I could call her all of the names under the sun, this wasn't about her, it was about him and the fact he had chosen someone else over me.

So I did what I always do best. I put my head down and pushed myself back into my career path. Unfortunately I had to leave the Canberra Ship due to medical reasons. Whilst I was on my first ship the Tropicale I fell asleep in the Sun when we visited Venezuela and the skin on my face was very badly burned and there was one mark that wasn't healing so I went to see the Surgeon on board and he signed me off at the next port because he thought it was skin cancer. We thought at the time I would have need to travel to London for the surgery but was very lucky because one of the top Maxillary Facial Plastic Surgeons at the time for St Thomas's hospital was performing surgery in Swansea, again go figure? How lucky was that but truly it was a blessing? They removed both lumps one from underneath my left eye and one from my lip. I had fourteen stitches in total and yet you would never believe it if you saw my face now. Once again I thank my parents for good genes. I was signed off work for almost two months during the healing process and was bored out of my mind. Derek had heard from his mum that I was home and what had happened to me and of course he called me to let me know he was home and wanted to see me. I went out for drinks with both him and his parents that night, after all I was still friendly with them all. I still had the plaster over my stitches and was pretty embarrassed about it. Derek being Derek told me I was still beautiful and took the band-aid off my face. We left his parents in the local pub and went on into town for some Indian food. We sat there for hours talking and I guess all I wanted was answers as to why he married someone else, only he couldn't answer me. There was sadness in his eyes that I could not explain or understand? Was this the look of regret or the look of pure apology for hurting me in a way that was unrecoverable? This was the night that Derek and Muriel were created. He is the one that created them, not me. He was always shy in telling his true feelings and didn't feel comfortable at all so this was his only way of letting me know how he truly felt. I'm not going to share what was discussed because that is personal to me but take my word for it, you would cry if you hear what he'd said to me.

We decided to go back to his parents and we sat chatting practically all night, until we both fell asleep on the sofa. The next morning I got a cab home whilst he was still sleeping, I couldn't bare to say good-bye to him, not again and especially seen as what I now knew that Derek had told Muriel. He called me a little while later at my parents to say how lovely it was to see me and then returned back to his wonderful little life in London.

A few weeks had passed and I received a phone call with an offer I could not refuse. The company was taking over the sister ship of The Canberra and I was asked to be a part of the opening team to do yet another world cruise, only to actually travel around the world in the opposite direction than I had the year previous! As you shitting me? I'm 21 and now I get to cover the continents I missed out on about six months ago. This truly was a dream come true for someone as young as me. Of course I jumped at the chance only this time I actually went on board as Assistant Manager through promotion and I absolutely loved it. There were some familiar faces in the crew that were also on the Canberra. The ship was a lot smaller than The Canberra also but I didn't care it was a lot more quaint and yet had such amazing character. The world cruise was divine; I covered lots of different places that we didn't get to see on the other one i.e. Solomon Islands, Singapore; Mauritius, Italy, Brazil, USA, South Africa, Gibraltar etc. It was phenomenal.

Now, interestingly enough I did make friends with a Chef on board who we will call 'Psycho' because this was one weird man. I decided I could either be miserable for the rest of my life or I might as well at least try to move on. Derek had. How come when you fall for someone you only ever see the good things yet once you know they're not for you the faults are illuminated? Wouldn't' it be great if there was a textbook for guidelines on what fashion disasters to look out for on first dates and what they mean? My mum always told us to check that the person we are on a date with has clean socks on. At least you'll have an idea of what kind of home he comes from! This guy was English; we'll leave it at that. Beautiful looking and quite shy actually, a bit like me! O.K I'm belly laughing here, we know I'm far from shy but there was something about him I really liked. He finally plucked up the courage to ask me out on a date and we had our very first one in Hong Kong, quite romantic or so I thought?

Now, you have to understand that working on a ship you only ever really see people in their uniforms so I'd only ever seen him in his Chef's Whites as they call them, apart from the odd night in the crew bar in shorts and a T-Shirt. Well, oh my Friggin god, get the fashion police out because this gorgeous man didn't have a clue how to dress? He walked off the gangway and had pinstriped jeans on, white socks and SHOES? No? Don't shatter my illusions on this cute guy. I made him walk as fast as he could so that no-body saw us! The next stop in Southampton I made sure we went shopping ha! This guy was lovely to start with; adored me and would do anything for me. The ship went into what they call dry dock; that's when it's raised out of the water to have repairs done to it before another long stint of cruises but it also means no electricity or water so all crew have to leave. I even invited him down to meet the family and I also went to stay at his in England, I met some of his family but they weren't very friendly to me at the time. I just put that down to them being Londoner's. When we got back on board he started to get overly jealous for some unknown reason. I'd decided to lose all the weight I'd gained and was working out like a maniac and he thought I was doing it for some other man? He would get access to my cabin whilst I was in work and rummage through my drawers under my bed and in my wardrobe. All of my photos were pulled off my wall and cut up to shreds? He cut up every card he'd ever bought me and threw them all over my bed. This completely freaked me out and so I had no other choice but to end it. I tried to be civil to start but in the end I had to go to his department head because when we returned to the ship after dry dock I had received promotion to Spa Manager so was now a department head on board and this was unacceptable and embarrassing for me. It got so bad that it actually reached the Captain of the ship and we all had to arrange a meeting to try and come to some sort of conclusion. My decision had been made. I wanted to leave the ship; he was making my life hell and I just wanted to get as far away from him as humanly possible.

In the end I really don't think I had a choice. I spoke to my company at the time and I received a transfer out to the US on a rinky dinky Tonka toy of a ship called 'The Festivale'; which was again another Carnival Cruise Ship. I nearly died when I saw how small this thing was and how small the salon was on board but let me tell you I had one of the best teams I have ever had on that ship. We broke every revenue record since inception and the whole team got on like a house on fire. I only stayed on there four months and was then transferred to Alaska on a Norwegian ship, The Wind. I hated this period of cruising; Alaska was beautiful but the ship was full of people waiting to die; I mean I think they were actually older than god half the time. I could not wait to get off but believe it or not I actually ended up extending my contract due to the fact the money was so great. I went home pretty exhausted if I remember and all I wanted to do was sleep. I'd worked ten months straight without a vacation. I spent the whole time in Wales with my family and pretty much loved it.

Of course, it's like as if Derek had his very own personal GPS link to me because as soon as I would be back in Swansea he would call me and say 'guess where I am'? Of course he would say he was sitting in his mums kitchen or words to those effect! We hung out a few times whilst I was home; which I hated myself for but I just couldn't say no, I just could not let go of this unbelievable connection we had. I took two months off again and then decided to go back out to the Caribbean on a ship called The Imagination, Carnival Cruise Lines again. I loved this ship with a passion and was very successful on there as far as work goes. Now, during my contract on this ship I started to get very friendly with the Host on board; which was the Cruise Director. An American guy, lovely looking but a bit full of himself at the time, or so I thought. I had decided to take a break from dating after Psycho because it was just hard work. He called my parents telling them he was going to fly out to the Caribbean and bring me home from the ship I was working on at the time, mum's response was simply 'don't waste your money, she's not interested'. He continued to hound my parents for months after and kept sending me threatening faxes; it was out of control. So when the CD came along, we'll call him this for short because I can't bare to actually say his name out loud or in writing; which you will learn why soon. When he started to pay me attention I made it very clear I wasn't really interested in seeing anyone as such but we could be friends. Over the next few weeks we did become friends and got to know each other quite well. I would pop to his cabin for lunch and after work before he did the shows in the evenings on board to say hi but nothing more. The more time I spent with him the more I got to see how much drive and ambition he had and to be perfectly honest he was like a male version of me; that was the best way I could describe it.

He had all these grandioso plans of making as much money as he could to eventually open up his own agency. CD had been married before and divorced; to an English girl believe it or not. That didn't bother me really because right at this given time I found myself falling for him and everyone has a past right? I got to know the person first; which was even better and now not only were we best friends we were lovers also. I thought I had died and gone to heaven. I was so very, very happy. For once, work and relationships were on the climb. We had so much fun getting to know each other and of course with him being the main voice for the cruise I would always get extra marketing plugs for the Spa on board. Miami was our Home Port on a Saturday and I'd been to visit my corporate office to hand in my weekly paperwork but when I arrived back on board the phone in my cabin was ringing; it was one of my team members who was also a very good friend of mine at the time calling to say that CD was being taken off the ship?

What? I took the elevator up to his cabin and he told me that he had been suspended for a reason I still do not know to this day? Great, now what? Two minutes of happiness to be snapped back up in the blink of an eye! CD left the ship that day and I didn't probably see him for at least 2 months. I called him from every port and it cost me an absolute fortune. After a while he found out he wasn't coming back to this same ship he was being transferred and asked me to go with him. It was a big decision to make but it felt right somehow? I got my transfer about a month later and we tried to pickup the pieces as best we could. It wasn't easy and I will tell you that I did think I had made a huge mistake after I got there. I should have just gone for a vacation with him first and looked at the ship but no, not me, dive in first think about things later! Silly cow. I hated this old rust bucket. The clientele was horrendous and all we did was sail back and forth to Nassau in the Bahamas for four months. GET ME OFF!!!! I finished my contract early and could not wait to get home. I was truly unsure of how things were going to work out with us but he invited me out to stay in San Diego during our vacation and we actually had a lovely time. I got to meet his mum and his friends and we just relaxed the whole week I was there. During this time we both decided to try and get back on the same ship again as each other which we did. The Carnival Holiday was our next little escapade! I'd worked on that ship for a very brief stint a few years back so it was quite a nice thought to get back on there. The ship sailed to Mexico and back basically; I didn't really care too much for the Itinerary at the time as by now I'd pretty much covered everywhere I the world I wanted to go except Antarctica and I wanted to go there on vacation not work so that would wait. I love Mexico. It has to be one of my most favorite countries on this whole planet. I love the people, their version of Spanish as a language; their culture; the religious beliefs but mostly their food. I LOVE GUACAMOLE! I seriously thought I might have turned green by the time I got off that ship ha ha! Things were great between CD and me for a while; yet work wasn't the best. The ship was very old and it was due to go out of commission not longer after that stint so they filled the last few weeks with the cheapest cruises possible; which meant your average person wasn't spending money in the Spa; they wanted to keep it for Alcohol! Guests were urinating in the elevators and stealing from the shops on board; it was dreadful. I was experiencing cruising hell. The next bombshell hit us. The situation that went on with CD on the Imagination was never closed and unfortunately he was taken off yet another ship. I was upset naturally. I had chosen to go on a shitty little ship for him and now I'm stuck here on my Jack Jones. Alone again naturally! The good thing about this disaster though is we sailed out of L.A and San Diego was only 1+? hrs away so he used to come and see me once a week for the first few months. Then CD decided he was going to move to Vegas; a great opportunity had presented itself to him and he didn't want to turn it down. Vegas was still within distance for him to drive to L.A once a month; even though it was a four-hour drive. It was hard only seeing him for the day but I knew we would see each other once my contract was over, which we did. He found this cutest apartment there and I actually stayed with him for a few weeks. The interesting thing here was that at the time my company were starting to merge into land based operations and were believe it or not planning on launching a property in Vegas! I was actually considered for the project at the time but the plans fell through. Another competitor company managed to steal the deal so I was actually offered a position in London as Recruitment Officer. I was kind of like an ambassador of the company and would sell the job of working on cruise ships to potential candidates. It was a very difficult decision for me at the time but I wasn't able to legally work in the US so I had no choice; I had to go home. We continued to have a long distance relationship for a while but it was hard. We would constantly fight over trust issues and did result in us actually breaking up for about a month but then lo and behold I got sent to the US and Canada to recruit and took some vacation time with CD only by now he had left Vegas and moved to Lake Tahoe for work. It was my first trip to Tahoe and I have to say I absolutely loved it. It is such an amazingly breath taking place. CD was working selling timeshare; which he wasn't very good at and he struggled financially up there but in his usual fly by the seat of his pants way he managed to get by. My work aspect of this trip was very successful, so much so that I was offered a position to relocate to Miami! I could not believe it; it's what I was hoping would happen and what I told myself would happen. Another prime example of the saying 'Be careful what you wish for because it might just come true'. Well I had been putting this wish out into the Universe from the start of my role in Recruitment. Each and every college I visited I simply told them I wouldn't be in the role very long as I was relocating to Miami; this was prior to me even asking for the transfer. Well it worked because now here I am planning the next stage of my life only in a completely new country also.

One thing I was nervous about was telling Derek. We'd been speaking on the phone and texting again whilst I was based in London and then I did actually see him one night. My stomach was doing summersaults thinking of how I would bring this out but he kind of made it easy for me. You see, once again in his presence I melt and we ended up spending time together only he never called me after that day. I was kind of expecting it really; the time we spent together was pretty magical but extremely emotional at the same time. I hated the thought that I couldn't have this man in my life; I hated the world for taking him away from me but I knew that when he was with me; he was truly mine. Truth is; I knew deep down in my heart that he loved me back in a way that no one else has or will ever be able to. I just knew I wouldn't hear from him again; he couldn't leave the life he had and the only way to stop feeling the same hurt was to stop communicating with me. Yes, once again here I am devastated. I sent him a letter and told him I was moving; he never responded; I took that as my closure. He could never come out and tell me himself he thought I was doing the right thing or that it was over because of what he said to me that night Derek and Muriel were created. I knew he would never be able to tell me it's over between us; those words will never come out of his mouth whilst he is living on this earth. I never told CD that I had been in touch with Derek; CD knew that Derek was my 'one true love' and would always bring him into our conversations if we argued at all. He knew that there was a part of me that always loved Derek. I couldn't help that, you don't get to choose who you fall in love with and in my case I was still very much so in love with someone I couldn't have. O.K; I'm starting to fill up with tears now because I did really love CD but I wasn't sure if I was 'in-love' with him. I wasn't settling by being with him I was trying to move on with my life and thought at the time I was 'In-Love' with him but there was still no way of letting go of my memories and feelings for Derek. So off to Miami I go!

CHAPTER 10

US of A here I come!

In December 1999 I moved to Miami. A big decision I know but one that I felt was right from the start. A few weeks later CD joined me; he decided to leave Lake Tahoe and try to find a job in Miami. We found an apartment when he arrived what with me being so new to the US he pretty much took control of everything. We purchased a car and started to try and begin a new life together. We had absolutely no furniture apart from a bed and a dining table and so we had to start from scratch and build on making it into a home as the months went on. We didn't end up staying in that apartment for very long due to the fact it was infested with Termites and for those of you reading this who is not 100% familiar with what Termites are; the best way I can describe it is maggots with wings! Oh my god; they were gross. The whole apartment was falling apart where they had eaten right through the woodwork. We moved further south into a Townhouse; it was lovely. It was a bit of a commute to work for me but worth it. The friends we hung out with at that time were all living close by so it worked well for us. CD was still struggling to find work; or should I say was quite happy being a man of leisure! To me he just seemed as if he didn't want to work. Every day he would go to the Internet Café and scour for jobs but would still come away with not even as much as an interview. After a while this became extremely frustrating for me because I never thought I would see this side of him. What happened to this awe-inspiring person I fell for? CD was like a completely different person and I had absolutely no idea what I was going to do about it. Every time I brought the subject up it was like I was placing him on trial in court; he completely freaked out and would storm out of the house. We went for weeks on end not talking. Eventually my boss at the time helped him get a job doing the same thing as what I was doing but for a different company and of course he hated it. The truth is he had just lost his whole drive and ambition only he had no explanation as to how; why or what he was going to do about it.

To add salt to the injury things were pretty tough for me with work. I was completely loving my new job in Miami yet was having a hard time with my boss. You think after watching the 'Devil Wears Prada' movie that there's no way on this planet that someone can be that evil; well I will have to disagree with you. My boss was ten times worse. The real sad thing about this though was that she had no reason to be miserable. She was successful; financially secure; beautiful home; fantastic car, amazing clothes but was very lonely and didn't want to see anyone else happy. She was very territorial at the time; whether that was her own insecurities with work I don't know but everything I did I took great pride in and wanted to grow but she would keep you in a position that was of no threat to her. Everyone respected her for what she had managed to accomplish in her career but the lonelier she became the more she would turn into this nasty person. In the past she has actually given me the most amazing career opportunities and I have her to thank for a lot but the more efficient I was becoming in my role the harder she made things for me. Then the trip that changed my life and relationship with her was about to take place. We were scheduled to go to Cozumel in Mexico for a week with each other to visit ships that sailed in and out of there. The first few days started out well but every evening we would go for dinner and she would drink so much wine that I would have to practically carry her to her hotel room. One night I had to undress her and place her PJ's on! Then on the very last night of our trip she was so drunk she started opening up to me about some very serious secrets that she was holding onto; one of them being the fact that she was still very much in love with someone in the company that she'd had a relationship with but had since married someone else. They had dated for quite some time and yet he had chosen to marry this other person. I think at the time this truly did break her heart and she could not come to terms with it but covered it up well until now. Although there were rumors flying around that she completely trashed his office after he dumped her. She completely let her guard down and I remember feeling quite sorry for her but was almost in shock a the fact she chose to share these emotions with me and as much as I felt sorry for her it made me nervous because I'd seen what she was like with other people she had come close too. My gut instinct was that this was going to go horribly wrong somehow and I was right. She always had a history of embarrassing herself with alcohol and was actually removed from one of the company Christmas parties because she could barely stand up. The next day we met for breakfast and it was like I was sitting with a complete stranger; she could not even look me in the eye and did not say a word to me the whole journey back. I don't think she remembered everything we discussed but obviously she remembered the most important parts. I felt physically sick and was absolutely dreading what would happen when we returned. It was a known fact that if you pissed her off in any way she would either fire you or send you out on a field trip for a month at a time and I was sent to Alaska! From that day on there was nothing I could do right in her mind and she simply made my life a misery. Now one thing you need to know about me is that I can come across as being a tough cookie on the surface but ever since I was a child I would bottle things up inside and come out in a face of cold sores as I told you earlier. I suffered extremely bad with them and would get them on my face, lips, neck and breasts and I have to say that on more than one occasion they have been so severe that I look like I've been in six rounds with Mike Tyson; blisters and scabs all over my face and they would take sometimes up to six weeks to heal. The situation with my boss went to the next stage and I was so overwhelmed with stress and fear of my future that I ended up losing my hair; I had two patches of Alopecia and to this day they still haven't grown back properly. I lost so much weight I just had no idea what to do. CD was very angry with me because all we would talk about would be work and her; it did put an immense strain on our relationship at the time but I just didn't know what to do. I was fearful that I was losing my job at the time and was too scared to tell anyone but like every bad situation there was a silver lining. I didn't want to leave the company. I truly did enjoy working for them then news came that the company had just completed an acquisition for a chain of land based spas throughout the UK and I decided that I would apply to work for them. I thought at the time it was my only way to keep my position in the company and to stay in the US with CD. I think my boss, as much as she didn't like the fact I applied it was an easy way to get me out of her way and of ever spilling the beans.

The months following were extremely stressful on both of us. CD's mum had recently found out that the Cancer she had recovered from years prior was back only this time she chose not to go through Chemotherapy and face the consequences of doing so. Her health went down hill dramatically and within six months she sadly passed away. I was unable to go to the funeral because of work but I remember picking him up from the airport and he was devastated. He didn't want to go back to the apartment right away he wanted to go sit on our favorite spot on the beach where we sat to see the New Millennium come in. As we sat there he spoke about the funeral and how lovely it was and how much it made him realize he needed to cherish the special people in his life and with that he went into his pocket and brought out a box! Oh my god, I could just remember thinking 'is he going to propose to me'? Yes, I was right! I was gob smacked at the time; I just could not come to terms with the fact he had done this during such a sad time but he wanted to bring light into the family and this was his way of doing it. The ring was pretty, a lot smaller than I had ever hoped for. I knew he was going to propose at some point because he had shown me several rings to see if I liked any of them but this one was a 1 Carat Diamond Platinum ring with Baguettes' at the side. How could I say no? This was official; I was getting married and the whole journey back to the apartment in the car, all I could do was think about Derek. I wondered what he would think when he found out. There was a part of me that thought perhaps this was for the best, this was the closure I needed with him but there was another part of me that thought if I did marry CD would I prevent us ever from reconciling. I chose to try and forget him and didn't even write to him to tell him, I chose to move on with my life without him in it. No matter how strong I was trying to be at the time by trying to move on, something in my heart just told me 'this is not going to happen, you will not marry him'!

Believe it or not a few months later I was granted my transfer and moved across to the West Coast of the US and was based in Los Angeles managing a Spa in Beverly Hills. Both of us were excited about the move because it meant that CD would be closer to his family and right in the heart of the Entertainment Industry; which is where he really wanted to be to progress in his career and I had the chance to succeed without the pressure of my last boss. The only problem was that when we did arrive to L.A after resigning from his job in Miami he once again lost all motivation and was quite happy to lie around all day. This took a major toll on our relationship and things just got worse. I had a major hissy fit one day and told him that if he didn't find a job our relationship would be over. He did listen and found a position in a Golf Club. It wasn't perfect but was a great way to meet influential people. I was relieved in a way that he did find a job; not only financially but the fact it helped us to try and recover our relationship for a while. I still held a lot of resentment inside me though; I couldn't understand why he didn't want to provide for us. In the beginning we really did struggle for a while and yet I was busting my butt trying to make my career a success. Everything went over his head and nothing seemed to faze him. I was reaching the point of anger that turns to resentment and hate actually. I just hoped I would be able to get through or passed these emotions though and every day it was getting harder and harder to pretend.

Christmas was just around the corner and my parents had invited us to stay in Wales. I was so excited because it was years since I spent a Christmas at home. CD was looking forward to it also but then when he requested time off his company would not grant it, after all he'd only been working there for a few months. Together we made the decision that he would leave that job take the vacation home and then find something when we returned. My parents were just thrilled at the thought of us going home and her and Dad came to collect us from Heathrow airport in London. We arrived home two days before Christmas. Mum was so excited; she had the whole trip planned.

KICK START THE BROOMSTICK

Christmas Day she was expecting 25 guests. CD told my parents on the journey home that his oldest friend since childhood was living in London and that he would be spending the Holidays on his own. My parents wouldn't want to see anyone on their own at Christmas so they invited him down to stay also. His friend arrived on Christmas Eve and we decided to stay in and have a few pre-Christmas cocktails. Mum and me had laid the table ready for the next day before both her and dad went to bed and left us sitting in the kitchen to catch up. I went up to the bathroom and as I walked back down the stairs I could hear his friend asking him what he was going to do for work when we returned to L.A and the next few words he spoke changed my life forever. CD responded to his friend and said 'why would I want to find a job when Ang earns great money'? I felt physically sick and just stopped in my tracks and started to shake. How could I possibly put on a brave face and pretend I hadn't heard what I did? I composed myself and walked back into the kitchen. I made up some excuse that all of a sudden I felt tired and was going to hit the sack. What I didn't realize at the time was that my mum was out the laundry room and also heard his comments. I walked up the stairs and went straight into the bathroom. I was crying at the same time I was trying to take my make-up off; mum walked in and gave me the biggest hug; she didn't say a word and walked back out but that was her way of telling me she heard; I knew she had because she came up the stairs after me. This must have been so difficult for her. He climbed into bed and tried to hug me but I pretended I was sleeping. I remember crying myself to sleep silently that night not knowing how on earth I would be able to get through Christmas Day with a brave smile on my face. I just wanted to beat the shit out of him; I was so angry yet would most certainly have won the Oscar for my performance during the rest of the trip. Nobody would have ever detected anything. Christmas Day was a mixture of phenomenal joy from spending it with my family yet sorrow of knowing what I did. The rest of the vacation is all of a bit of a blur; I just couldn't wait to get home and face the inevitable.

We flew back to the US on New Years Eve and had an overnight connecting flight in New York City. We had originally planned to hit the City with style to celebrate New Years Eve but I found myself once again faking being ill and said that I'd had severe stomach pains that was probably food poisoning from the flight and so we stayed in the hotel room and slept. The next day we arrived back in L.A and I was faced with yet another huge reality; the division I had relocated to L.A for was being sold and I was to fly that week to Miami to meet with God to discuss the options for my career. I met with the President of the Resort Division at the time; oh boy this man was just amazing; I was so inspired after meeting him that I hoped I would be able to join his team. I did actually get the job and was so happy and it also meant that I would be relocating back to Miami if I wanted; he did give me the option to stay there if I preferred. All I could think of was just get me as far away from CD as possible. I remember flying home to L.A after some intense traveling of almost three weeks. I landed around 11.30pm and was expecting CD to pick me up only as I came through baggage claim I saw a sign with my name on it; he'd sent a Limo to pick me up and take me home and there was a message on my phone to say that he had gone out with the boys. I was furious but it just added fuel to my fire. L.A was eight hours behind the U.K at the time and as soon as I walked into the apartment I called my parents to let them know I had arrived home safely and to tell them of my news with work but the biggest news I shared was that I had decided to call off my engagement and was going to end my relationship with CD. During that phone call mum confessed that she heard the conversation and shared this with Dad also and that if I decided to go through with the breakup her and dad would support it. Dad was so upset; he really did like CD and was shocked to hear how much he'd hurt me by the things he'd said but after all I was his baby girl and no one would ever come before me in his eyes. I think Dad was disappointed more than anything.

After spending more than one hour on the phone with my parents I remember hanging up and all I could think about was Derek? I just wished I could talk to him; he always managed to put me back on the right track and make me feel better so I decided to write to him and tell him what was happening in my life. For some reason the letter just flowed and I think by the time I had finished it; it was fourteen A4 pages long. I remember putting my business card in the envelope and sent the letter to his work place as I always did. I wasn't sure I was doing the right thing; we hadn't spoken in almost three years at this point. I never in my life thought he would have responded and so what did I have to lose? CD arrived home around 4AM; I was so tired but refused to go to bed until I had spoken to him. He walked through the door completely buzzed on Alcohol and actually thought everything would be O.K with his cocky, arrogant way that he had sent a limo to pick me up. I remember sitting there and just thinking shit or bust I'm just going to tell him. I sat there and told him it was over and that I would be moving back to Miami on my own. Of course in his cocky way he thought I was joking and that tomorrow I would change my mind? What he didn't realize was that everything he'd put me through made me fall out of love with him. I couldn't bare him anywhere near me; the thought of him touching me made me physically feel sick. We didn't get to bed until 7am following our discussions but he slept in the guest room. I woke around 12 and came into the room to ask if I wanted to order Pizza? Are you shitting me? I think I threw the nearest thing I could at him and he stood at the door and said 'oh, come on Ang, your still not going on about breaking up, come on, we'll be fine? Let's order Pizza, have a glass of wine and watch a movie'? I burst into tears and remember screaming at him and throwing something. He just didn't get it. I showered; dressed and drove to Publics storage to purchase boxes for moving. When I arrived home and started sorting through things, I wrote CD on his boxes and AB on mine. This was the moment he started to understand that I wasn't joking anymore. The sad part about this was that he didn't even try to fix it.

That night we both slept in the same bed, with me underneath the covers and him on top and around 2am the phone went; it was my cell phone. I was too tired to pick it up and so left it go to voice mail but he wanted to check it just incase it wasn't anyone from Wales with a problem. He hung up the phone and I asked who it was, his response was 'some Welsh guy saying a joke and that he hopes you are O.K'! Oh my god; it was Derek; he called and I was too tired to answer. Probably just as well at the time because I wouldn't have been able to talk to him but at least he heard my cry and wanted to check up on me. I remember lying there thinking about him; wishing he would call back but he never did. The next day CD was all inquisitive thinking that I had decided to end it to be with Derek? He proceeded to say that I had never truly loved him and that it was only a matter of time before I ended things with him. The next few weeks were exhausting and so very emotionally trying. I think I dropped seven pounds in weight within a space of ten days and had a face full of cold sores; yet he didn't seem to care. He had decided to move back to San Diego and planned on staying at his best friends. The day the movers came was tough; I think I cried all day and then he drove me to the hotel that I was staying in before flying back the next day. He was meant to stay the night with me but chose not too; he wanted to just head back as soon as he could. Looking back, it was for the best. The next day I stood outside LAX Airport in L.A and just felt free. I cried the whole journey back but was relieved that I had finally made it. I found an apartment on line but it wouldn't be ready for three weeks; the same time my furniture was arriving so I stayed with a very dear friend of mine who helped me transition back into my new life. He was a bit of a lifesaver actually; he made me feel so welcome in his home and also helped me with my move into the apartment. I simply adored him and what helped was his sense of humor; he just made me laugh all the time. I have some great memories of that time I spent with him. I'm sure I completely got on his nerves but he never showed it.

So, there's me thinking that finally I have a chance to move on with my life and forget about the disaster of a broken relationship I had just experienced but no; CD was not going away that easy. Due to my intense travel schedule I managed all of my house hold bills on line and then one Sunday night I was transferring money from one account to another when I saw charges from California? CD and I had a joint account; only it was just my money going into the account? That was when I realized he was still using the bankcard and had taken money out of the account. I called him to ask him why and his response was 'what do you expect me to do, I have no money'? I could not believe what I was hearing. I went to the bank the next day to get him removed from the account and unfortunately I needed a Notary from him and the bank in order to remove him. Once I received this I took it straight into the bank and hoped that would be the end of it but it wasn't. Over the next few weeks he completely cleaned me out and took everything from both my checking and my savings account. Here

US of A here I come!

I was Twenty-seven years of age and had to start fresh with zero in my bank and there was absolutely nothing I could do about it. I was devastated as you can imagine and don't ask me how I managed to get the strength to come through this but I did. I just knew that if I got my head down with work I would make back the tens of thousands of dollars I had lost and so that's what I did. The sad thing was he came from a very wealthy family and not one person, not even his dad offered to assist me at the time; they all knew what a loser he was. That should say something to you.

Aside from the additional stress I loved my new life back in Miami. I had great friends; a great social life; great apartment; life was good. I didn't date for close to two years after our breakup; I just didn't want to be around men. I wasn't a man hater or anything I just didn't want one in my life. Miami was a very difficult place to meet people anyway; it's a very superficial city and all about what car you drive; what job you have and how much money you have in your bank account. Being somewhat attractive it wasn't difficult for me to meet new people but as soon as the men I met realized I did actually have a brain and an opinion of my own I would never hear from them again. A lot of men are threatened by successful women and only want 'Trophy Girlfriend's' on their arm so the minority of us would be banished from that category; me included. I decided to take a different route with dating and try Internet Dating! Now, if you haven't already had a giggle reading this you are about to. I decided to set up a profile on Match.com. It took me a few months to pluck up the courage to actually meet someone in person but my first date was with a Maxillary Facial Surgeon. Oh my goodness here we go. We had arranged to meet in a place called Lincoln Road; great restaurants and bars only at the time I wasn't really into Sushi and yet he insisted on meeting in a

KICK START THE BROOMSTICK

Sushi/Thai Restaurant? As I pulled into the car park he called and explained he would walk towards me to collect me and as I turned around I could see this tall guy who looked from afar as if he wasn't half bad then as he approached me I nearly died; he had the worst Toupee on I had ever seen in my entire life! You could even see the bobby pins that it was held on with. My jaw just hit the floor. If I was like any other person on the planet I would have just ended it right there but I just didn't have the heart. I haven't been brought up like that so I decided to stay. I felt sorry for him actually believe it or not. Anyway he had booked a table at a restaurant called 'World Resources'. How could I possibly sit there and avoid being recognized was all I was thinking? It was such a popular place to hang out. I asked the waiter to sit us at the side of the trees so I could at least try and hide behind it and I explained that I wanted it for intimate reasons! I had already come up with a game plan in my head that if I didn't have appetizers or desert I could make a sharp exit and put it down to being tired and an early start the next day. I just picked at my entree and really didn't eat any of it. My plan worked and so we asked for the bill. The waiter asked if I would like to take my leftovers home with me and I explained that the only leftovers I do is cold Pizza and then all of a sudden my date proceeded to tell the waiter to box if for him; he wanted to take my leftovers home!!! I think my chin was grazed instantly where it hit the floor; I was mortified and couldn't wait to get out of there. As soon as I got in my car I could not stop laughing at this man's wig moving every time he ate his food. I was laughing so hard that I couldn't possibly keep it to myself and so I pulled over onto the hard shoulder of the freeway and called Donna Wonna; of course with the time difference I woke her up but to hear the laughter on the other side of the phone was well worth it. Donna always said my dating stories would put the British Soaps to shame.

How embarrassing was that and to top it off I received yet another email off the same guy months later asking me if I would like to go on a date? He clearly didn't remember meeting me; ever; I obviously made an impression on him didn't I?

It took me a while before I decided to go on any other dates and for very good reasons. When I did decide to try again I spoke with the guy for probably four weeks before I plucked up the courage to meet him. Coffee; let's just do coffee, that can't be difficult right? Wrong, I arrived at Starbucks in Miami Beach and saw this guy waving to me; I walked over and once again he looked absolutely nothing like his photo and only he had his own hair but sadly he didn't have his own teeth! His dentures were so big in his mouth that they were moving as he was talking! I couldn't make this shit up even if I tried honestly. Disaster again. I was starting to think I was being set up on 'You've Been Framed'. That was it for me for Internet Dating for quite some time. You see; once those situations happened to me I simply fell back into work mode again and gave up trying. I have always been married to my career and found it very difficult to meet anyone who could accept that. Why is it so hard for some people to accept that a strong, confident businesswoman can actually be a very loving and gentle person deep down? Of course I did what most single women did; I thought there was something wrong with me but I realized that wasn't it. Being a great believer in fate I just knew that there was someone for me; my 'Knight in Shining Armor' was around the corner, only I think he fell off his horse! That was my excuse and I was sticking to it. My famous last words when a date didn't work out….NEXT!

CHAPTER 11

Devil In Disguise

So, back to my career it is. Aside from being single I actually loved my life. I loved my new job in the Resort Division and truly felt as if I had found my 'Niche' if you will. My boss at the time was such a wonderful mentor but he never made things easy for us; he always challenged us to find better solutions to situations; which actually helped us grow in our profession. I had the wonderful opportunity of setting up start up businesses in Mexico, Puerto Rico and the U.S. The hotel property's we launched in were off the highest quality so it truly did make our job a lot more pleasurable especially as we would be away from home on site for the whole build out at times. I was in Mexico for almost three months but loved it. Well; most of it. I did have a trying time whilst I was there. Not only did I break my wrist on that project I lost two grandparents; my mums mum and my dads dad all within three weeks of each other and due to the fact I had plaster on my arm I was unable to fly home for any of the funerals. That did not impress my mum as you can imagine but there really wasn't a lot I could do about it. It was a very sad time. Not long after that project I was sent to Puerto Rico with one of my very dear friends who was due to be the Director of the Spa. Oh boy this was a test let me tell you. Mexicans speak a completely different dialogue of Spanish than the Puerto Ricans so everything I had learned on the previous project went out the window! What a great place to shop though; I turned into a shoe whore down there but it wasn't long after this project that the next one was happening in Orlando.

Boy was I tired of traveling! To anyone reading this you'd think I had a perfect life and there were some really amazing perks with it but the truth is I didn't really have a life; I was married to my career and it's probably the reason I'm still single today. Well, partly the reason. I did love my job though; I'd been with the company for so long that I had managed to become quite successful. Now, unfortunately my boss resigned from the company and little did I know what such an impact it would make on my life? For a while he wasn't replaced but then it happened; the Devil came to work for the company as my boss. This man had an existing relationship already with the company and all I could think when I knew he was going to be my new boss was 'holy crap'! He was the most arrogant person I had ever met in my entire life and was nothing but a complete sleaze bag. He'd slept with half of the team he was affiliated with and fired the ones that wouldn't. I have to say I did panic because I just didn't know how he was going to be with me due to the fact he had already told me on more than once occasion in past meetings with him that he preferred to work with men. Well he started and let's just say that holy hell broke out. I've never been spoken too so badly in my entire life; his aggressive behavior was just out of control. He just didn't know how to speak to people. Between he would shout all the time, that and his disgustingly foul bad breath I thought I was just going to die. When he first came on board with us I had to take him to the properties to introduce him to everyone in the team. We were traveling together for almost a month and at one point I nearly got on a plane back to Miami; due to the fact I've never met such a rude person in my entire life. This man was rude to everyone; cab drivers; hotel staff; everyone! One night at dinner he actually told me that a new sheriff was in town and if I didn't like it then I knew what to do. I was simply devastated and nervous all at the same time and yet once he'd had a cocktail he would start getting too close and try flirting with you. I could think of nothing worse than to be with someone as disgusting as him; he literally made my skin crawl and I hated every bit of time I had to spend with him. I told my senior boss what had been happening and he did try to intervene in the beginning but I think it was something he really didn't want to be doing; he didn't need two leaders of a division fighting? I really tried to work with him but every day he would find faults somewhere along the line and always make sarcastic comments to me about how he was the boss and don't ever forget it. Now, what was worrying to me was that I had just bought a new apartment on the Miami River; I was so scared I was going to lose my job so I started working on my resume and found some great head hunters that were helping me and then lo and behold I got promotion to Vice President of the Division? I was seriously surprised. I knew I deserved it; I'd worked my ass off for 18 years for them but once I did get it I was expecting things to get better; only they got a lot, lot worse.

I don't know if he was some how threatened by my new promotion or what but he just turned into a very evil person from that moment on. The sad thing was that he also turned several of the team members against me also. I dreaded going into work to a job that I had adored for so long. Such a shame but there was nothing I could do. I tried my hardest to make things work but it got so bad that he would go days without even speaking to me; he gave me the silent treatment yet would speak to everyone else around me in front of him. The only time he would speak nicely to me was when he wanted to know what my ideas were and then he would go straight into God's office (that's what I used to call the big boss) and he would literally take the shine for every suggestion I gave him. I completely and utterly resented him for that; I truly thought that god would have seen through it but he didn't. Unfortunately god didn't and he had his two sidekicks that would feed him with jealous negative information about me and I think he lost trust in me in the end.

What was even more sad and truly showed his insecurities to me and my role was that we would have several meetings set up with business partners and he would invite me along and then change his mind just before we went into the meeting? I would be asked to wait outside? What on earth was that all about? I felt so stupid at times and in the end I would just not go to them. He stopped all of my team communicating with me directly; they had to go to him. What he was trying to do was strip me of all my power and was enjoying it. I overheard a conversation he had with one of my team members telling them he was relieving me of some of my duties because I was overwhelmed and couldn't cope? I wanted to punch his face in let me tell you but of course, once again he held all the power. If we were traveling he still held all the power; he had absolutely no manners; most men would open the door for you; help you with the luggage; give you a little bit of respect; not him; he was so rude and god help us if he was drinking; he asked me and one of the staff to take him to a strip joint! I couldn't believe what I was hearing; honestly; he was nothing but a complete sleaze bag always rubbing your arms and things like that. He even asked us to take him to a strip joint one night; which I did report to HR when I returned but it fell on deaf ears. He fired one of my team in the past because she wouldn't sleep with him and I knew this before he was hired but thinking back I should have told God about it but I trusted him and didn't want to be disrespectful to his position. I just wasn't going to win with this guy. December came around and it was time for our appraisals; we had to do the self-appraisal first and from there they would sit us down and review it. He actually told me that he had been given the go ahead several times throughout the year to fire me if he wanted too but that he liked me as a person so I can stay! I was devastated and didn't know what to do; can you imagine being told that and then trying to perform? I walked out of that office and just felt sick. I decided to go and speak to HR and see if there was anything I could do. The HR Director just sat there and took it all in; she didn't really give me any form of sense of job protection what so ever; she just told me to try and talk to him. I was leaving the next day for vacation and was off for 18 days. I thought maybe the time apart from each other might be what was needed. I knew I didn't feel comfortable leaving without talking to him because I didn't want to go on the Christmas break feeling like that; especially because I was actually hosting Christmas Day this year but I just didn't know what to say. I tried not to think about it and put on a brave face. Christmas was a huge success. I had the ugly jumper competition; we had musical chairs; Karaoke; and each guest had to bring a decoration to hang on the tree. We truly did have a fantastic time. I always got nostalgic and missed home terribly; I would cry like a baby to my parents on the phone but the family I now had in Miami were wonderful. I loved them all.

So January comes around and we head back to work. The devil was being his usual arrogant dick head self but I just put my head down and decided not to bite anymore. On the Wednesday I received a phone call that I never thought would happen. My mum called and told me they had detected breast cancer in her right breast and she would need to have a Mastectomy it was that serious. I nearly dropped the phone; I don't think I have ever experienced an emotion like this before and just didn't know what to say. Of course I had so many questions and didn't know where to start but most of all was concerned for mums well being; bless her; she was trying so hard to be strong for me on the phone but I was on my way to work and promised to call her that evening. I hung up the phone and went to pick the Devil up to head to a meeting in South Beach, Miami because his car had gone in for a service. I was crying as I picked him up and told him about the phone call but he was emotionless; all he said was 'you've got to do what you've got to do' when I asked him if he thought I would be able to take some FMLA time off; that means Family Medical Leave Act; which protects you and your job as an employee and allows you to take the necessary time off. He said he would speak to HR for me and would get back to me. I got home that night and called my mum; we found out that she would be going in for surgery in two weeks and so I just asked her to stay strong and I would let her know what HR come back with. Friday morning I got called into the Devils office and HR were sat there; I thought it was to discuss my mum, wrong! I sat down and he said that they had decided to let me go; I was being FIRED!!!! This was all down to the fact I had gone to speak to her about my appraisal. I couldn't believe what I was hearing; I just couldn't think straight. I was given 5 minutes to clean out my office and then I was escorted from the building…ESCORTED FROM THE BUILDING!!!! I was simply mortified and devastated at the same time. I hadn't even owned my apartment for a year and had worked with them for 18 years; what was I going to do? I called my parents immediately and my dad just couldn't believe it. Legally they were putting themselves in a very serious position but I still think that to this day God wasn't aware of my mum's situation or my HR request, as I'm sure he wouldn't have let this happen. What kind of person would want to put someone through something like this knowing what I was already dealing with? Only the Devil. I got in my car and under normal circumstances anyone who had just experienced this would have gone home and cried their eyes out; not me though I went straight to Office Depot to buy a laptop and as I'm there Janet one of my best friends called me and said I could borrow hers for a while so I drove straight over there to pick it up. Janet was amazing to me that day; she was so unbelievably helpful and sensitive to my needs. She made me sit down and write a long 'to do' list so that I had a focus when I left her house. I remember getting home from her place and within 3 hours I had reached out to several headhunters and emailed my resume to almost twenty companies on line. Around 6pm Natasha called to see me at home; she was one of my other very close friends only we had known each other the longest as we used to work on a Cruise Ship called the Canberra. Tash was devastated when she walked into my apartment; she just couldn't stop crying and didn't know what to say to me; nobody did. I had the most amazing friends out there and everyone pulled together for me.

The next night all of the girls came to mine for Wine and Pizza and somehow tried to support me. Corinne was wonderful; she allowed me to print my resumes at her house so that I could mail them out to companies and she also helped to put me on the right recruitment tracks for the US seen as she was American. Janet is Irish and Tash is English. The three of use were so very different; Tash was called Carrie because she was a shopaholic like her only she had red hair; naturally curly with a crazy personality; so much fun and yet really gullible, she would believe anything you told her bless her. I actually lived with Tash for a few weeks whilst I was waiting for my apartment to be ready, we did have such a laugh. I taught her how to cook a baked potato correctly can you believe that? It actually worked out well for us both;

I cooked her dinner every night and she let me sleep in the guest room; I'm sure by the time I left she was glad to see me go but she never once showed it. I remember this was the time we found out Tash's dog Kye Spencer could smile! I'm not kidding; we would be out all day at work and when we walked into the apartment he would separate his lips but keep his teeth closed and it seriously looked like he was smiling. We couldn't stop laughing. The sad thing was; Tash had to place a bark collar on Kye because as soon as she left he would sit by the door and bark at everyone getting in and out of the elevator and so she received official complaints from the Management company in her building; she had no choice but to place this collar on him poor thing.

Anyway back to the job thing or 'No' job I should say. I spent the next week planning a trip home to Wales; I figured if I'm not working I might as well be home for mums surgery and recovery and I can look for work whilst I'm there via the internet. Mums surgery was very stressful as you can imagine; we didn't know what to expect and it was a lot worse than we could have ever imagined. Mum wanted us girls to take her to the hospital and as we were sat outside on the bench she kept telling us all how much she loved us all and how just incase anything went wrong for us not to forget about her. This was absolutely heart wrenching and I still to this day don't know how we managed to stay so strong for her. I had only flown in that morning and then here we were taking her in for one the most difficult surgeries of her life. After we said goodbye we all went up to Allison's house for a glass of wine and sat and laughed and cried all at the same time. The thing was, everyone in my family was slightly in shock with me, they couldn't believe I'd lost my job. My dad was so upset because he didn't see it coming at all. He could see what they were trying to do to me (the Devil and his two sidekicks) but he thought God would have been able to read through the lines but he didn't. Dad was so upset about this and was worried for me obviously but the whole time through mum's recovery at home I sat on the Internet searching and searching and searching for jobs. I think I sent my resume close to 50 different companies hoping that someone would bite.

I stayed in Wales for almost a month and truly didn't want to leave but I knew I had to find a job and so I flew back to Miami. Leaving my mum was probably the hardest thing at the time; she didn't want me to go and was crying at the airport but she understood the severity of me not having a job at the time. I hated myself for leaving but had too. I cried the whole journey home and was just mentally and physically exhausted by the time I walked into my apartment. I just felt sick; I'd probably dropped at least ten pounds in weight through the stress of everything but me being me didn't stop for a breather. As soon as I got back I was on the job hunt again. My god, looking for a job was a full time job; I'd spend fourteen hours a day searching through websites. My problem was that I wanted to stay in Miami and the jobs were limited there for what I was looking for. As strange as this may sound my heart was still sitting in Wales though.

Now that I was home I tried to keep my regular routine as much as possible and every morning I would go for a run outside around the area that I loved and always passed St. Jude's Church. Without fail I would walk in and light a candle for mum and for me to find a new job. I had also reached out through prayer when the devil first started being difficult to me but I guess the universe had other plans for me. I wanted something local; if I didn't have to travel that would be a bonus so that I could finally start having a life again. I knew I wouldn't stroll straight into a company as Vice President but I was going to try my best to stay on the same salary; at the end of the day I had a huge mortgage.

After a few weeks of being back I did manage to find something amazing. It was in the Medical field and I absolutely loved it. This was the first time I had worked in the Medical field so it was a tremendous challenge. Now what was quite strange is that both my boss's practiced in some kind of Witch Craft. It was strange how I would be drawn to working there. The people were wonderful and not having to travel was a dream come true. Unfortunately the recession hit Miami pretty badly and we ended up letting go of so many staff; that was the part of my job I hated the most; honestly.

Then March 13th 2009 my sister Donna called me to tell me that my brother Terry was taken into hospital and that they didn't think he would make it out? I couldn't believe what I was hearing and felt as if I had a million questions but just didn't know where to start. I went into work the next day to let them know just incase anything happened and I had to fly home. Of course I couldn't concentrate anyway. 5am Saturday morning my mum called me to tell me the news; my brother was in critical condition and was being kept alive by the machines but the doctors had decided to turn them off because all of his organs had collapsed. I think I went deaf and when I realized what she was saying, I was begging her to not let them turn off the machines until I arrived home but it was too late; he had already gone. My big brother; dead? This was not how things were meant to be? He has six children; he can't leave them? I was simply devastated. I text my boss to let him know and I booked my flight for that afternoon. I had to arrange for Sooty to be taken care of; my friend looked after him for me. I was in such a daze going to the airport; I took two sleeping pills and slept the whole way home.

CHAPTER 12

Thirty-Seven

Thirty-seven? All my life I was told by the spirits that my life would change when I was thirty-seven. I thought it would be when I finally met someone; either settled down in a relationship or had a baby? Never in my life did I expect to have a complete change. You see, the day I arrived in Cardiff Airport for my brothers funeral something inside me changed; I knew I probably wouldn't want to go back to Miami and I was right. I walked into my parent's home, took one look at my mum and just lost it. Truth is, I hadn't really settled back in Miami since mum's surgery and all of my friends knew this. I had been thinking about moving home for quite some time and was ever so homesick all of the time; crying and not sure why? But this very day I knew my life was about to change forever. Over the next few days I spent some time seriously thinking of what I was going to do, I just didn't have the answers and so I went for a Spiritual Reading to see if I could get some guidance and right enough my grandmother came through and so did my brother. My Nan couldn't understand why I was dragging my feet and not putting the business idea I had in my head into action? Of course the idea I had meant leaving Miami and moving home to set up my own business but my concern was losing my apartment and Nanna told me that 'you can't take your apartment with you when you go to heaven but you will take your soul now it's time you started living'. She also told me that she would be right at the side of me to give me signs along the way but to not doubt myself because if I chose to do this it will be very successful and you won't need to worry about losing your apartment; another one will come along to replace it. My brother also told me in the same reading that I've done what I set out to do in my career and now I should be proud to take a step back from the fast paced life I had been living for twenty years. Now its time for me to settle down and start living the life I couldn't throughout my career. Terry also told me that I will have a lot of words to put in writing but not to worry as the spirits would be my inspiration; only I couldn't understand that comment at the time but now look at me; I'm writing this book! So much of what they said to me hit home. I had been so unbelievably miserable for probably the last four years I was out there. Don't get me wrong; I loved my friends; the lifestyle itself with the weather etc. but there was always something missing only I couldn't quite put my finger on what? Of course my immediate thought would be relationships; all of my friends were dating at this point excluding Angela but I think that was her choice at the time. Of course you ask yourself the age-old obvious question 'is there something wrong with me'? I knew there wasn't; having the gift that I do I knew it was all about timing and somehow it just wasn't my time I guess. Either that or I'd been a complete bitch in a past life with men and Karma was coming back around!

You see, Eight months before I finally decided to leave Miami I was sat on the sofa messing around on the Internet looking for wholesale items to sell if I was to open my little store of infinite possibilities and I came across a company that was called 'Something Different'. After scouring their website I was pleased to see that they offered pretty much 70% of the items I wanted to sell and so I emailed them to see if they shipped to the U.K. I wasn't sure what country they were based in and I received a response from the owner of the company back within the hour; which really impressed me and he advised me that yes; they do ship to the U.K. but he could do even better than that because they were actually based in Wales; in a city called SWANSEA!!! Oh my god I nearly fainted! That is my hometown; are you kidding me? That was sign number two; the first one was from the spirits. I remember calling Donna Wonna from my sofa and she couldn't believe it. Now what was so unbelievably odd about the timing of all of this was my car lease was due to expire at the end of April; my passport was due to run out in the August and it was as if the heavens were helping me to wrap things up to go home right?

So to be 100% certain and to get a fresh perspective, I decided to take myself to a little place on Lincoln Road for a Tarot Card reading, it was a gift given to me the Christmas prior but I hadn't used it yet. I wanted to try the Spanish lady for a change and get it translated for me, as I wasn't very impressed with my last one with the usual woman that did it. She was crap but the Spanish lady was spot on let me tell you. She asked me why wasn't I doing readings for a living? She could see that I had this business vision and that I should follow my gut instincts with it. She held her hands up in the air and said 'You could have a store like this'. Now my Nan also told me the same only she said if I didn't follow it I would lose my gift forever? That truly scared me; I couldn't' imagine living without it? She also told me that someone from my past would be coming back into my life but that could have been anyone at this stage if I was moving back to Wales.

Now I had already told my friends what I was thinking of doing in February 2009 at a friend's birthday party so when my brother passed away they honestly thought to themselves that I wouldn't come home.

Thirty-Seven

Tash knew me better than any of them and I guess she knew in her heart that I'd make the right decision to stay. All of the gang knew how close I was to my family and so I cant say they were surprised to hear my decision. What's really interesting to learn was all of the staff cutbacks at work that were being done; I was next so I guess everything happens for a reason right?

I flew back to Miami over the next few days and the whole time over on the plane I questioned was I doing the right thing? Of course I'm bound to do that right, after all Miami and the US had been the only life I knew for the past Twenty years. I had spent more time abroad working than I had lived in the UK so I knew it was going to be difficult for me to adjust but something told me I was doing the right thing. Now, it wasn't just me I needed to take care of it was Sooty also so off to USDA I go to find out what I needed to do to get him home. Sooty was my little black 'Psychic Shih Tzu'. Bad news; he wasn't allowed to leave the country for six months due to the Rabies Titter test he had to have done. I was devastated and just didn't know what to do? I looked into Quarantine for him but it would have cost me close to five thousand pounds for the six months and I seriously didn't want to waste money on that. Here's another great example of how amazing my friends are. Janet Martin also owned a Shih Tzu called Prada; she was adorable let me tell you. Janet offered to look after Sooty for me for whilst I moved back and got things sorted but at the time I didn't want to be a bother to anyone but now it looks like I will be more than grateful to take her up on the offer so I called her in hysterics crying and asked her if she still considered her offer and of course she did; she was absolutely fantastic to me.

Just to give you an idea of what Janet is like as a person; on her 40th Birthday instead of receiving gifts from her guests she asked them to all donate money instead to my mum's Cynthia Barnett's Think Pink Foundation and she raised close to $1,600; it was actually the highest donation we received. Who on earth would be so kind as to do that? We live in a selfish world but this woman was and still is everything but selfish; she truly is an amazing kind-hearted person. It's funny; I think I miss Janet the most because we had such great fun at her house. We used to have sleepovers for the weekend and I'd pretend I was going on my holidays for two days! We would always kick off Friday night with a fair few bottles of Verve Champagne and a Witchy night; I would do her Tarot Cards and she would do mine and lo and behold she has the exact same cards as me strange? Not to me it wasn't; it was just confirmation that we had so much more in common than we realized really. So the dog was one thing less to worry about but boy; bloody expensive the whole process I think cost me close to $3,500 in the end. Now it was time to get the Apartment on the market and get bids for moving. I knew this wasn't going to be cheap either but there was absolutely no way was I going to sell my furniture after all; I'd custom bought it and shipped it all from Mexico. I loved my belongings and was not prepared to leave them behind. In between meeting with respective companies I decided to start going through the cupboards and drawers and throwing things away that I wouldn't need any more. Now baring in mind I had only lived in that apartment for two years; I had so much crap it was untrue and I think I must have cleared around 15 black bags with nothing but junk in them. Anything worth keeping I gave to one of the girls I used to work with as she was moving into her first ever apartment with her boyfriend bless her.

It took me almost three weeks to pack up the apartment and shed many tears along the way also. It's funny actually because I always dreamt of owning a New York style apartment and as soon as I saw the

Thirty-Seven

floor plan I knew I would fall in love with it. My only regret with that place was not waiting until the building was up and running so that I could have gone to view the apartments at night to review the soundproofing. It was horrendous; I could even hear my neighbors having sex; it was gross. It was extremely frustrating for me at the time; I was very disappointed with this but there was absolutely nothing I could do about it. I could hear my neighbors phone ring; them coughing; and of course the TV! I hated that part. Aside from that it was lovely, right overlooking the river with great restaurants within walking distance. Sure I was going to miss it but still, I felt as if I was doing the right thing. So; all of my friends wanted to plan a special leaving party and we decided we would do a BBQ at Angela's building; she has the built in community BBQ's around her pool and we had such a fantastic day. I was absolutely wasted and lost count how many drinks I had that night; I don't even remember taking Sooty out for his night time walk but it was worth it. I remember sitting around the pool thinking how very blessed I was to have such fantastic friends but I knew they would always be my friends, even if I was just a plane ride away. I had decided to spend my last week with Janet to get Sooty settled in his new home for the next few months. I took Sooty to Janet's the day before the movers were scheduled to arrive; I didn't want him to see what was going on. I knew he would have completely freaked out and would have been more difficult for him to settle after I left. That night without him was weird; I guess it was a test of what was to come for me. I remember waking up early so that I could wash the bedding and pack it before the movers came, only when they arrived I just felt sick. I just didn't know what was going to happen with me. For the first time in a very long time I felt lost; even though I knew what I had set my sights on I still felt unbelievably lost. Now; strangely enough the

123

day my movers came was also the day I had to take my car back to the Dealership; two major things to let go of all in one day. I was a wreck. Janet came to the rescue once again and drove down to Miami to pick me up from the dealership and take me to her house. We sat there that night and drank lots and lots of wine. It was quite nice for me to do what I did; I kind of relaxed for a few days before heading home to a crazy few months of setting up a new business etc. More importantly I got to spend some quality time with Janet and the dogs; it was fun.

O.K so the day has come and it's my last night in Miami. I was dreading the next day. I just knew what was going to happen; I would say goodbye to Sooty and then instantaneously fall apart in the cab. I was up early that morning. I don't really think I slept much anyway. Janet had gone to work; we'd said our goodbyes the night before just incase she didn't have the opportunity to come home during her lunch break. The dogs were playing as usual and I sat in the kitchen and probably smoked ten cigarettes whilst I was killing time waiting for the car to pick me up for the airport. I never smoke in the days; I absolutely hate it but today I needed a sedative of some kind and that seemed to fit the bill. The cab arrived and the driver came to the door, took my luggage and placed it in the trunk. I picked Sooty up and it's as if he knew what was going on; he just looked so sad to see me leaving again and cried a very unusual whimper as if to say 'bitch; you're leaving me again'? I couldn't look him in the eye as I closed the front door for the very last time; locked it and threw the key in Janet's secret hiding place. I got in the cab and was absolutely balling my eyes out. I felt as if my heart had been wrenched out of my chest and I was just sobbing uncontrollably. I called my parents and my sisters and of course they tried to calm me down but it was to no avail; I needed to cry and get this off my chest. Call it therapy if you will? I arrived to the airport in

Thirty-Seven

Ft. Lauderdale only to find out that my first flight had been delayed; which meant my connecting flight was going to be tight. I was sat in the airport and called my mum; I was ever so emotional and as always she was right behind me telling me it was all going to be O.K. I knew it was but just needed to breath and come to terms with things. All of this was my decision; I had to follow my gut instincts and the signs from the spirits. They have never let me down before and won't start now so brush off our shoulders; peacock feathers up and let's go start a new life in Wales.

CHAPTER 14

Croeso Y Cymru: Welcome To Wales

So, here I am sat on the plane with a glass of champagne in my hand toasting to myself 'here's to the first day of the rest of my life'. Secretly I was so scared it. I'd done so much in my life yet each new chapter never got easier to begin. My flight was fine actually; I had two connections to get me into Cardiff but we arrived on time. Now all the years I've been traveling the one time I need things to go smoothly they lose one piece of luggage on my arrival; of course it had to be the one with all my clothes in. Oh boy I was not a happy camper let me tell you. Eventually they found it, it ended up in Amsterdam somehow? Just as well I didn't end up there with it because the way I was feeling I probably would have tried a funny fag and never made it to my next plane. I'm just joking; I've never taken or tried any form of drug in my life. I'm bad enough on Alcohol and the odd Ciggy when I'm drinking is suffice. I've never been interested in drugs actually. Some of my friends have tried Cocaine when we've been out at parties but it never interested me. So here I am sat at the airport waiting for the wrinklies to come and get me. No doubt Dad was driving ten miles per hour as he usually did; you see I'm sure he still thought he was driving the lorry with work! They pulled up curbside with the car and we managed to get my one piece of luggage in. I had the warmest hug off my mum as you can imagine and Dad actually also. Donna Wonna was with them; I guess she thought I'd needed morale support right now and she was right.

Month's prior to making the decision to move home we had been talking about names for the store and Chriswick was Nanna's maiden name so with it being so catchy the 'Witches of Chriswick' was born. Nothing else was done but it was a start. I remember landing at 8.40am and at 12pm the girls had made arrangements for me to view a property that had the retail space and apartment above it. Instead of going to Allison's where I was staying we decided to go to mums for a coffee and toast. We all sat there kind of in disbelief that I did actually go through with it; I have moved back to Wales and yes, it was FREEZING. Donna had seen my move back home in the cards and told my mum a few months prior that I would eventually be back home only she didn't believe it and to be honest with you all; if my brother hadn't have died I'm not sure I would have plucked up the courage to do so; as miserable as I was. Sometimes fate has a funny way of giving us a nudge. So it's 12pm and Allison, Donna and I went to see the property. I had such a funny vibe about the store; I had already worked on my floor plan prior to even walking in the store and when I did I couldn't believe what I was seeing. The way I had laid it out it up was to fit perfectly with the layout of the existing business. It would need a lot of work but that was something I was prepared to do. Off up the back stairs we go to view the apartment. I loved it; it kind of had a lofty feel to it because the kitchen and living room was all open plan, one big room. The bedroom was a nice size and then to my surprise there was an attic; oh my goodness it was just like my bedroom in my parents house all those many moons ago and it was perfect. The whole apartment had wood flooring excluding the attic; which was carpet. I knew I would have to make some functionality changes and my biggest fear was fitting my furniture in but it could be done. I told the real estate agent I was interested and he explained he would speak with his client and get back to me. I waited, and waited and waited some more until in the end I was getting 'slightly' frustrated. Problem with me is I have absolutely no patience what so ever and I want things when I want it or not at all. He came back with a NO, that the owner was considering using the property for something else? Oh boy, if he did. We were furious that night and then Donna reminded me that we knew the person who owned the building so we reached out to him personally and managed to actually speak to him. I explained what my business plan was but he wanted to have the weekend to think about it. After I put the phone down and told the girls about my conversation they seemed to think I had it in the bag; I'd sold myself to the boss and more so because he was such a successful business man that had actually started his empire in Swansea that he might want to give someone else the same chance he had been given all of those years ago.

Now of course at this point though I didn't want to put all of my eggs in one basket so I spent the whole weekend searching the Internet looking for new properties just incase. I couldn't find a thing, not a bloody sausage. Was this also a sign? Sign or not, the pressure was on me. Monday comes around and my phone goes; it was the boss and I guess the 'good-guy vibe' was right; he offered me both the retail space and the apartment! I was bouncing off the walls at this stage as you could imagine. The space or the apartment wouldn't be ready until 6-8 weeks time; which gave me plenty of time to source the materials; products; finalize the business plan and my furniture to arrive from Miami etc. First things first, let's get on some British Business Courses to see what the variation is from managing in the US. Aside from the obvious one being pounds and one was dollars; I needed to understand the rules and regulations, laws and legislations and most importantly the TAX and NIC (National Insurance Contributions).

Over the next few weeks I placed myself on quite a few courses to kill time. I was staying with my sister Allison whilst I was waiting for my furniture to be shipped; that cost another arm and a leg. I loved staying at Allison's; her and the girls all made me feel ever so welcome and every day Sammy would pop her head in the bedroom and ask me if I needed anything bless her. By now I was missing my dog big time and would have a few tears as I got into bed each night I have to say although I tried not to show any of them. Allison helped me in more ways than one. You see I hadn't lived in the country for so long that I didn't have any credit at all so when the time came for me to try and buy a car or set up a new cell phone it was impossible. Allison came to my rescue with the car and I had to put a hefty deposit down to get a phone. I never thought it would have been that difficult to be honest with you but it was something I had to deal with when I first moved to the US so I guess there was no point in stressing about it. So I turn up for my first course and there's a woman there that I recognized her face? For the life of me I couldn't remember but I did ask her, I had too. She didn't claim to know me at all? The next day she came straight over to me and told me I was right and that year's prior when I worked for the recruitment division for my old company I apparently interviewed her and offered her a job? What a small world isn't it? She didn't take it due to having a boyfriend at the time and had now decided to open up her own business. I actually enjoyed the courses; it's always good to have a refresher with things isn't it? Nearly there. Purchased a new car; of course I had to get the same as I had in Miami a little black mini convertible and called in MJ2; that stands for MOJO 2. You see, I had a MOJO in Miami and actually had a naming ceremony party for it; everything was mini; mini quiche; mini baby bell; mini crackers; mini champagne bottles etc; but the reason why I chose MOJO was after Austin Powers; if ever I parked the car and couldn't remember where I

129

would have to say 'I've lost my MOJO'; well I cracked up saying it to my friends; they all thought I was completely nuts but loved the idea all the same. I had to wait for almost 7 weeks for my car to be delivered. Oh boy, I felt like I had lost my arm and truly did hate relying on anyone for anything. My parent's were great also; they took me to look for a new sofa; washing machine; condenser dryer; fridge and freezer only my dad doesn't really have the patience for shopping and so you would have to rush around the shops and get back to the car prompt-ish! In the end mum and me would go alone. You see; I wasn't used to having to buy electrical essentials; they always came with apartments in the US; why do we have to be so bloody difficult in the UK; another few grand going out of the bank!

By now I was starting to feel a little restless; I'd just found out that the apartment would be ready in two weeks; which gave me enough notice to arrange with the movers from the US a suitable day for delivery as they were already on the container in the middle of the ocean somewhere; they just needed the final destination address. I had a few days to kill before everything came together and so I hired a car and ran around buying all of the last minute items I knew I would need. There was also method to my madness as to why I hired a car; my brand new Mini Convertible (MJ2) was due to arrive and I guess I wanted to practice driving on this side of the road again after spending so much time in the US. So, it's 8am on Friday morning and received a phone call saying the movers were half hour away. I was so excited I could burst; finally having all of my belongings around me again and my own little space back, I couldn't wait. It took the movers almost five hours to unpack the lorry and bring everything in. Dad brought me food over and then mum came and made the mover's lunch, as I didn't have a clue how to use the new cooker, that and the fact I didn't have a clue what was in each box. I just wanted to unpack as many boxes as I could so that they would take the trash with them when they left. Selfish I know but another thing I miss about the US is the trash shoot and the skip in each building if you needed to dump anything. My dad helped me a great deal by taking things to the skip here for me. I hated going up there; it's located in a pretty dodgy area of the city and stinks. Call me a snob but I so don't care. After a few hours of unpacking things were starting to look and feel somewhat normal, my place was slowly coming together and it actually looked quite lovely. My sisters decided to come down that night and help me unpack although they seemed to enjoy the balcony more with a few drinks. They did offer to help but as you've already probably guessed; I'm pretty fussy with how I like things and knew where everything went so I would pop out every now and again to sit and have a drink with them but then it was back to it. The only strange thing was that believe it or not, my furniture and all of my belongings fitted into this apartment absolutely perfectly! It's as if it was meant to be mine. It wasn't my apartment in Miami but it would be home for now.

Over the next few days I continued to unpack and sort the attic out. You see, there were no wardrobes so I had a friend put some clothing rails up there for me and I turned it into a walk in closet if you will; it was perfect. Then one night I was sat up there going through the last few boxes and my cell phone rang; I didn't recognize the number and it was late so I let it ring. They hung up and rang again; and again until in the end I answered it and all I could hear on the other end was 'you don't know who this is do you'? Oh my god guess who it was? Yes, it was Derek. As soon as I heard his voice I hung up; I didn't know what else to do, I think I just panicked? I waited for ten minutes to compose myself and then called him back. He was in town and was once again sat in his mum's kitchen and decided to call me. First question out of his mouth was am I seeing anyone? He was only in town one night and insisted on coming to see me? I looked a mess; scruffy jeans on, a linen shirt and had done nothing with my hair but I thought oh well, tough shit! So in walks this person and I swear to you he is just like fine wine, it gets better with age. He walked up the stairs to the apartment and I could not believe my eyes; instantly I had the most amazing vibes from him and as soon as we hugged each other all I could think was 'he smelt divine'. Believe it or not we sat up until 9am talking and catching up on the last ten years; that's how long we hadn't been in contact for so there was so much to talk about and catch up on. I don't even remember feeling tired; all I remember is thinking 'will someone please pinch me'? Is this man really here? You see; a few weeks prior to this night we were sat in my sister Allison's house and Donna Wonna came up to me in the kitchen and said 'the spirits had just told her that Derek was going to come back into my life soon; but in a big way'? Of course I didn't believe this, not after such a long time and most certainly not now and besides I wasn't even sure I wanted him too? I was starting a new life here in Wales and didn't want anything to get in the way of that and I knew if I saw him it would probably distract me again like he always did. I felt like I had stepped back in time sitting on my sofa and I could not stop looking at him; he was simply beautiful still and like no other person on this planet could still make me laugh like old times only his jokes were not as funny.

I did tell him that but he didn't believe me. It truly was wonderful to see him though. Unfortunately he had to leave that morning; he had some pressing engagement at home and so just as quick as he walked back into my life, he walked right back out; or so I thought? We decided to stay in touch as friends; which I agreed, after all nothing was going to become of this right? He hadn't been gone an hour and he was back on the phone. Now, again Angie being Angie really didn't give a damn about how I was with him. Apparently he had become quite successful and well known in his field but to me he was still only Derek and take all the success away he was still that same person I knew way back when. It was as if time had disappeared because here we were right back in that same place.

We chatted for ages and then he continued to text me the whole journey home where we were just winding each other up as normal. I'm sitting on my sofa thinking 'what am I doing; this is going to go horribly wrong as it usually does'? Over the next few days the texts came more often as did the calls and then he asked me to go see him; he was traveling with business and asked me to meet him and so of course I teased him and asked why? All I can hear is this coy voice on the receiving end being stumped for words. Now, I told him I wanted time to think about this as I truly was unsure if I should but there was something inside me saying go or I'll never truly find out if we do still have that connection or not? Of course I called my sisters immediately and told them to come and see me but didn't tell them why. As soon as Donna walked into the apartment she knew he'd been to see me; she felt his energy all around me and knew something was about to happen. Allison pretty much said the same thing only she is always the cautious one out of the three of us and basically told me to be wise with my decision due to the fact I had a lot on my plate with setting up the business and simply didn't need the added stress or pressure. Neither of the girls was truly surprised; I guess they always knew in their heart that this man was for me and would come back into my life at some point. Donna always told me that one-day we would be together and there's something that you don't know yet but when Nanna O'Conner was alive she actually saw my wedding to him. One day she called my mum and dad around and told her of her vision but also told me I changed my destiny by moving away? I guess for my own piece of mind I decided to go. I was so unbelievably nervous I felt sick; my metabolism was on over drive and I stopped for food twice on the way up there in the car; I just couldn't stop eating. My tummy was rumbling the whole way up there! The closer I got to him in North Wales the more nervous I became but it felt right. I pulled up to the Hotel where he was staying and had arranged to meet him in the bar. As I walked in with luggage in tow there he was with a baby blue shirt on and jeans. Oh my god, he looked delicious and of course so did I ha! I had made the effort big time, my hair was lovely, and I'd been on the tanning bed and had a very pretty black dress on. Although I always made the effort for me, not for anyone else really?

I felt lovely if you know what I mean? He looked ever so nervous bless him and for the first hour did stutter on more than one occasion; I guess he was just as nervous as I was but I have to say I was shocked by this. You see; as I said earlier we both lived with our parents and therefore had never experienced time together alone and so it was kind of a lot of pressure; I felt as if I was sixteen again! Once again we find ourselves talking non-stop for hours; it was wonderful catching up with him. So much had happened in our lives that neither of us knew where to start really but of course knowing how quiet I am he couldn't get a word in edgeways as usual! We ordered room service that night and played music on my laptop that reminded us of Twenty years prior when we first ever met; sipping a beautiful bottle of Red Wine from Chile that I brought with me. All I can say is it felt magical. He couldn't quite believe all that I/we as a family had been through and was quite humbled by it. I guess he didn't realize how lucky he truly was in his life at the time yet had admitted to taking things for granted and wished he could have been more of a positive person. I found this interesting because it just goes to show that no matter what you have or how successful you may become, happiness has to come from the heart and I guess that's what he was missing? The very next day he had to go into work so I took myself off into the town for lunch and to do a spot of shopping. I found this gorgeous little French Patisserie and sat in for lunch. My phone was off the hook as you can imagine with my sisters wondering how it was going. After lunch I strolled around the town; it was very cute and lots of little different stores where I picked up something for my business. It was a little music maker that looked like a typewriter and the teddy bears moved with the song 'It's a small world after all'- 'There is just one moon and one Golden Sun and a smile means friendship for everyone, though the mountains divide and the oceans are wide it's a small world after all'. This kind of freaked me out because here I am having travelled practically every continent in the world; over 130+ countries under the same moon and sun as Derek and yet here we are back under the same ones again, together. Weird? Nothing is weird with us let me tell you? I have had so many signs all my life about this man perhaps this would be the time, now is our time finally to be together? This did run through my mind the whole time I was shopping. Anyway I got back to the hotel and Derek came home from work. We decided to go into town for Thai that night and it was divine. As usual, between still working on his Blackberry all night and us laughing all through dinner we had another fantastic night. We decided to go back to the hotel and enjoy the wine I had picked up that day and so we are just sat there once again talking each others heads off until the bombshell drops that he is still convinced we are meant to be together but not sure if the timing is right now?

KICK START THE BROOMSTICK

Are you kidding me? After two amazing days, what? This is where I have changed; a few years back I would have probably still sat there but not anymore; I have changed and grown as a person so why on earth would I want to play second fiddle at this stage in my life? I wont do it and so the next morning before he woke up I packed my suitcase ready to leave and as he woke he saw me standing there. I don't think he ever expected me to walk away from him like I did but I had too. I got in my car and cried the whole way home. Of course I had to let him know that I'd arrived home safely and so I text him and went to bed for an hour; before long my phone was going but I just didn't know what to say to him? I knew this was all going to end the same way as it always did with me being heart broken and so what was the point? That same night was my mum's best friends 50th birthday party in the Casino; I really didn't have the head on for it but my sisters forced me to go if you will to try and take my mind off him. As we were sat having dinner my phone went; it was him saying how much he missed me already and how he was never going to let me out of his life now that I am back in this country. 'what we have wasn't something that happened over night and wont go away in a second' were his exact words and for the next four hours we pretty much poured our heart out to each other and there I was; failing miserably about sending him out of my life for good. Truth to the matter is that no matter what I say or do this man has a hold on my heart; I can't explain how it feels but imagine loving someone all your life and never being able to be with them? Take that pain and times it by twenty years and then you'll understand where I am coming from. I just didn't know what to do for the best. We did speak and text over the next few weeks and then it was almost two months before I saw him again, he just couldn't get away due to his schedule. I just didn't need the distraction, why now, why come back and throw me off track again? My focus really needed to be on my business not on him and so I did just that; got my head down to open my business. It was vital that nothing was to distract me at this stage but the problem was that every time I had two minutes to myself I would find myself thinking about him and there really wasn't anything I could do about it. My sisters are going out of their minds with this by now as you can imagine. All Donna said was 'I knew it'! Allison is always the skeptical and careful one with us, and so always stayed on the fence if you will, I don't think she was ever at all convinced that he was back 100%. I think she was more concerned that I would get hurt bless her but all she did say was 'follow your heart'. How can I follow my heart; I'm scared it's going to get broken again. I tried; I truly tried not to fall in love with him again but failed miserably as I had every other time before.

CHAPTER 15

Tick Tock on the Witches' Clock

So, finally I get the start date of when I can I collect the keys for the retail space and I am simply bouncing with excitement. Just so that you can understand who I as a person, I truly am a crazy woman on a mission when it comes to projects with work and knew that I would absolutely probably not stop until I opened the doors. I spent the next few days placing all the inventory orders to ensure we had everything on hand ready for August 1st; the official opening day. Donna and Allison came over my apartment every day for almost a week to ensure we were prepared with the spell candles and secret boxes. They were fantastic to me throughout this week and really had a lot to put up with because when I get stressed I seriously do turn into the exorcist and my head starts spinning. The problem is that I put so much pressure on myself that it's not acceptable to deliver anything half assed. Everything had to be perfect. I was desperate to get the shop open on time, not only from a financial aspect but from a mental standpoint also. I needed to get my teeth stuck into this project to keep me occupied and take my mind of Derek also. The day I picked up the keys my sisters and I went straight into the space and started ripping the carpet out and trying to determine the color tones.

By this stage I had already decided on the floor plan so pretty much knew exactly what I was doing. Allison and I decided to drive up to

IKEA in Cardiff to purchase all the fixtures and fittings and oh boy; what a task that was let me tell you. Her poor car was stacked from one end to the other but we did have a giggle. We had shelving sliding all over the place and chairs coming out of the windows it was hilarious but when we arrived home we realized we still needed more shelving so we did several trips that week to say the least. The great thing about being a part of a very large family is there is always someone who carries a professional trade that you need. Lucky for me two of my cousins are carpenters and painters so I pretty much had the store covered. My other cousin actually built the wishing well for me; I couldn't believe it when he offered. I seriously thought he was joking but oh my goodness; you should see it, it's simply stunning. It took him almost a month to build it; I'll explain the purpose of the well in a little while, not that I'm assuming you don't know? So for five days straight from 10am – midnight we were in the shop every day cleaning and trying to get it ready. We were absolutely exhausted every night and filthy dirty. I have no idea when the last time that store was even cleaned; it was absolutely disgusting. The business that was in there before us had been there a while so it was only natural it would be ready for an over hall. Facelift more like!

We made friends with all of our neighbors relatively quickly and everyone in the area made us feel so welcome. The Pizza place next door would send in food every night that we were setting up bless them; they were so very kind to us and would always give us a discount on food if we ordered from there aside from the freebies they gave us. Now, the location I decided to move into was in the outskirts of the City. The more work we put into the space the more I realized it was perfect. I've actually set up businesses all over the world but this one was different; this was mine and of course due to the fact I was funding it myself I was being tough on all my contractors and made them fight it out between themselves. Donna's partner Shaun was a great help with contacts, if there was something I needed he would be the one I would reach out too. Shaun hooked me up with a guy for my signage and business cards and it worked out relatively well actually. I had the exact idea in my mind of what I wanted the look and feel of the signage and the business cards and basically I wasn't up for negotiations on it. I had a vision of me and my brothers youngest girls dressed up as Angels and Fairies to make people feel comfortable when visiting the store or the website. My brother wasn't around to be a part of the project so I wanted something of him in there; this was the perfect solution. Thankfully Kelly was willing to do it and the girls were actually excited about it. We converted the attic into a studio for the photo shoot and spent a good few hours trying to capture the perfect shot. The guy was ever so patient with us at the time and did his best to entertain the kids. Of course I had no idea how the photos were going to come out. You see, everyone turned up for the shoot and of course they were all there with their own cameras trying to take photos, I felt sorry for the photographer. I don't think he would have been so patient if it wasn't for the fact he was Shaun's friend. Over the next few days I was presented with the final 'Official Photo' and I have to say it was everything I had imagined it would be and more, I absolutely loved it. The girls looked stunning, so unbelievably cute and I felt so proud that once again a part of my idea or vision had started to come to reality. That day we decided on the font for the Signage of the store and as it was all starting to take form it became even more exciting. Everything I had in my mind for the store was most certainly coming to life and I simply loved it. Don't get me wrong there were several times during this week that tested me to a point of exhaustion. One time in particular was when Allison and I had gone back to Cardiff to pick up more items for the store and I left the key to the shop with my cousin who was painting only he couldn't remember where he placed the key so here I am, its almost midnight and we don't have a key to lock the door? I tried my hardest not to get angry but it was difficult; I just had visions of me sleeping on the floor of the store to ensure nobody came in but then my other cousin came to the rescue and changed the locks for me. I felt so bad for my cousin who lost the key, he was so distraught bless him and had done such a great job painting the store how could I possibly be angry with him right? All was sorted now it's time for a shower and bed before the next day of pretty much the same. You know, it's just as well my poor little Sooty wasn't around for all this stress; he would have been so sad and stressed bless him.

So back to the grind, the girls came over the next day and we all sat around waiting for the shelving to be installed. We wanted to get this done before the carpet went in so that we could have a clean floor for the installation. Again my cousins worked their butts off to ensure it was all done on time and as the store started to take form we could see exactly where we wanted to place the retail items. A very good old friend of mine hooked me up with a fantastic deal on the carpet and installed it at no cost to me; I was so grateful for what he did. The carpet was basic but looked lovely against the rich firefly red walls and it truly felt warm. Now it was down to pricing the retail items and of course this was the fun part. It was quite entertaining watching Allison and Donna fighting over who was going to use the pricing gun, it was hilarious. Allison had changing the roll down pat with that machine, although it did nearly make it through the window on more than one occasion. You definitely needed patience with it; which was something Donna and I most certainly didn't have. Its funny actually, you most certainly do get to see the best and worst qualities in people under pressure. Myself included. My biggest challenge was realizing that I'm not in the corporate world anymore and therefore had to completely change my approach on how I needed to get things done. I was used to simply giving directions and knowing the people I worked with in the past we were just on the same page so things would get done quickly. I never needed to ask because we all knew what each other expected but now I'm in unfamiliar territory. When dealing and working with family they take as many breaks as they like and you cant expect miracles in return, after all they were helping me from the goodness of their heart, not because they were getting paid for it but let me tell you something, I wouldn't change it for the world because my sisters were fantastic. They were so happy to finally have me home in Wales their pride gave them the motivation to get the tasks done, not by me asking them. It's interesting actually because we did make a pretty phenomenal team together. There wasn't one situation that we couldn't overcome. No matter what was going on I would always consult with them both to get the best take on things and without a doubt we would always make the best decisions. Bill and Ben the fix it men they were; they could do anything! They even took the door to the attic off its hinges to take the Condenser Dryer up there for me because the deliverymen couldn't do it?

I wish you could feel the gratitude I feel for my sisters when writing this. Words can't express how very blessed I am to have such amazing women around me who not only support me but love me unconditionally through the hard stressful bitchy times and through the simple moments where we would catch each others glances throughout the day that would show each other in our hearts that what we were doing was right. As night time drew near one evening we covered the windows with Window Lean a product that blocks out the view from the outside and then wrote 'Coming Soon' and listed the Witches Have Landed and this created such a great buzz in the community. People were scared to begin with because of the name. I should say the skeptics were scared as the 'Negative Ninny's' as we like to call them thought that not only opening a store in a recession was suicide but also adding the name Witches to it would make it harder for us. I stood by my word and have not given up to this day. I knew it would create a bit of a buzz and get people talking so much more so than if I'd of called it some random boring name. Now; long days of twelve-hour shifts five days in a row can almost kill you; I lost so much weight; I think we all did. The one thing I looked forward to most was my goodnight text off Derek, no matter how hard my day had been it always put a smile on my face and made me feel appreciated and loved. Sooty wasn't there for me to go home too so this was kind of a fill in for now until my boy could finally get here. I was surprised at the texts off Derek; it was so unlike him to put the content in the messages as he did; they were so loving and sensitive I really truly couldn't believe they were coming from him. My only thought was that he must have been getting soft in his old age! Either way I didn't care; I loved reading them and so that's all that matters. I used to send him one of my quotes on a daily basis, he loved them in the beginning and I couldn't wait to see what his reaction to them would be but you can guarantee he would respond. I had to remind him at times to see if he had in actual fact read it but he would always respond. So, the inventory has arrived and all retail shelves are stocked. The signage is up all we are waiting for now is the well. When it finally arrived I was so happy with it; I never expected it to turn out so lovely. My cousin truly did a spectacular job with it and you can see he had put a lot of time and effort into making it perfect for me. It might have cost me a lot more than if I'd purchased one from a different vendor but the way I look at it is this is unique; nobody will have one like mine anywhere else in the world and that's again exactly what I wanted; I wanted a point of difference and this is what I got. All of our décor items we sourced from Charity Shops, Antique Stores and car boot sales and they all seemed to blend in nicely with the environment. The store was beginning to look exactly like I had hoped it would, 'Oldie Worldy'.

Let me explain the concept behind the store so that you can understand and almost feel as if you are inside it as your reading. I wanted to create something very unique, something that has never been done before in Swansea but I wanted to create it to work around our family gift. I had the ideas and inspiration in my head but wasn't sure if it was just a pipe dream or if it was in actual fact a reality waiting to be born. I wanted to create a store that would have people talking for miles around. I wanted to create the store that would fill the void in the community and have people coming from miles afar to experience it and see it. I wanted people to feel a sense of 'Déjà vu' as they entered and for them to feel a sense of calm that they would not want to leave in a hurry. How did I do that? This is how.

From the rich red and warm vanilla color tones of the walls that instantly brought a sense of warmth to your heart shadowed by the Cream Voile Drapes hanging in the store front window to the soft furnishings that made you want to sit and relax, especially on the Antique Chaise Lounge chair that immediately became a conversation starter with my clients to the Ivy that filled the ceiling wall edges to take off the sharp shape of the room; which softened and lowered the ceilings to a more inviting retail space as apposed to the sharp bright fluorescent lighting that was very much needed but not loved by me (only in the Winter). The soft Angelic music playing in the background hidden away from guests eyes to get their senses longing to find where this beautiful relaxing sound was coming from and the smell of Incense Sticks burning that immediately made you want to relax and just simply take it all in. Forget about the world for just that short amount of time you were in here with us and do nothing else but explore the history that now lived in a place we call home. A place that I like to call 'The Store of Infinite Possibilities'.

Scattered around the store we have the most amazing retail items for sale. We wanted to have items that were very different and that nobody else would have. I wanted my clients to want to like practically everything so that they would want to come back or tell another friend about it. Personally, I did introduce a lot of the items into the store that I actually like. I know my taste is different but I also know that the people in Swansea are obsessed with the future; they truly do get a major buzz from it. From Good Luck charms to Spell Candles; to Tarot Cards and Angel Oracle Cards which can be used for either daily messages or can actually be used to perform Past, Present and Future Readings. Of course I have the beautiful silk bags for sale to put your cards in to protect them; I have Tarot Cards and as you are soon to find out that my cards are actually twenty years old! Some of the ornaments we have for sale are simply adorable, from Fairies and Angels to Unicorns and Buddha's. Relaxation CD's, the same as the ones being used in the store and I always have a little sign saying 'Now Playing' so that the guests know which one they are listening too. Without fail I have a different incense burning all day every day and when the weather permits I have the door wide open where I allow the smell to waft out the door so that all passers by whether it be on foot or in a car with the windows wound down can actually smell it.

The amount of comments I get from guests as soon as they walk into the door is pretty phenomenal; it just makes them smile. Of course I wanted to cater for all ages so I have a wide variety of things for young children and new born babies also but the best sections I like in the shop are the 'Chill Pills' bath bombs and the 'Practicing Witch' section. Now for those of you reading this that don't know what Bon Bon sweets are, they are round little toffee candies covered in either white, yellow or pink sherbet and are simply divine. Well, the Chill Pills actually look like them and the amount of people that have actually put them in their mouth is unbelievable. Now, if you weren't offered a sweet would you just take one from someone's shelf? I wouldn't but the funniest person to do this without realizing it was our Postman. I have never laughed so much in my life. He came in as he does on a daily basis and as he left he said 'Oh, Bon Bon's; lovely, I'll have one of them; and so he picked up a white one and placed it in his mouth! No sooner was I about to say 'DON'T' he spat it out and realized what he had done but by this time I am in fits of laughter and can't speak to tell him. As you can imagine that very same day I created a sign that read 'DO NOT EAT'? Seems quite a stupid thing to do for us people in the world with common sense but you will be amazed at how many people in the world do not even know what that is. The smell of the Chill Pills is very powerful; I located them right at the side of the front door so as soon as you walk in you the odor hits you immediately; which triggers off a conversation starter.

The 'Practicing Witch' section is for exactly that. If you are interested in working with the Universe then you will love this section. We have everything from pre-packaged Spell Candles that can help you find Love, Pregnancy, Success, Protect Your Home, Banish Negativity, Angelic Help and also to win in BINGO! Most importantly we have a wide variety of Ingredients for sale that can actually be used for certain spells for either you to perform on your own or for us to personally put together for you. Either way; we do warn all guests that want to try this stuff to be careful because it does actually work and you know the famous saying 'be careful what you wish for because it might just come true'; well dabble with this stuff and sit back and watch the results, that's all I can say. Now, we do have some wonderful items for protection that you can use also such as sage and smudge sticks; menthol tabs and charcoal tabs to burn when practicing also. These are all great tools to keep your safe when practicing. Aside from this we have the Wicca Jewelry such as the Pentagram Circle; the Chalice; the Broomstick and The Witch. These make great gift items or wonderful personal 'From Me to me' items which I love the best! I do also have a very natural section yet still powerful; I carry over twenty six different types of crystals that cater for everything from depression to weight loss, anxiety to assisting with finding love! The biggest ingredient you need to have when purchasing any of these stones is 'Faith'. Now it's time to tell you what my favorite item is that we sell. It is none other than the 'Prayer and Protection Bracelet'. I first found these when I was living in the US. As you know from past chapters I used to visit St Jude's church quite frequently; every time I would run outside I would light a candle in there and one day the retail store was open inside the church and they were selling the bracelets. At the time I bought one for myself in hopes it would help me in finding a new job after I was fired by the Devil and then I ended up buying one for my mum and my sisters at the time mum had her Mastectomy. Of course once my mums sisters saw the bracelet they all wanted one as well so I remember getting home and having to mail about ten more back home for them and some of my cousins. This actually became such a valuable tool of 'Hope and Faith' to us during this challenging family time of mums cancer that I continued to buy them as gifts for my friends that I was surrounded by that I thought at the time could actually use it to help them. You would be amazed if you saw the look on the faces of the people I actually bought them for, absolutely a 'Master Card Moment' – priceless! Do you know that just by wearing them the people actually changed?

Call this coincidence; call it odd but whatever you call it you can't 'not' believe me when I say they have to be one of the most powerful things I have ever worn in my life. Let me tell you exactly what they are and what they look like. They come in many different forms of either crystal or wooden beaded bracelet that contain dangly charms of all different 'Saints of the World'. As you are probably aware a saint is a person recognized by the Church that has been particularly holy and/or touched by God, usually Catholic, but there a few others that recognize saints. They can come from any walk of life, but many have been some form of clergy at some point in their life. It takes decades to be recognized as a saint, and, of course, you have to be dead. If you look into the history of some of the world's most famous saints you will find that it took almost twenty five years for them to be recognized by God but each and every one of them were made famous for something they did for humanity such as St. Jude, the Patron of Impossible Causes or St. Christopher, The protector of Storms and Plagues or St. Luke, the Patron for the poor and Socialite Justice or St. Theresa, the Patron of Headache Sufferers or St. Angela, the Patron of Dedication to Education for Single Women (go figure) or my favorite St. Valentine, the Patron of Love and Marriage. The list goes on and on but this special bracelet contains charms of twenty-two different Saints so just think how powerful they are for you to wear them? I actually tell my clients that when you wear them, not only will you feel peace in your heart it will also give you hope that things can improve in your life but watch this space as amazing things miraculously start changing in your life for the better immediately upon wearing it. You may not be able to understand at the time why they happen or when they will happen, but just have faith that it will happen. I never walk out of the house without mine on unless I have my running gear on and don't fancy whiplash off the charms! This particular piece of jewelry I import and simply can't keep them on the shelf; I always sell out within weeks of receiving them. I've just introduced a new style also; which is the same style bracelet but instead of Saints as the charms they are 'Angels – Cherubs'; these are for more of the comfort needs or people who just want the protection of Angels around them, not to be used for a specific cause. They are so cute; adorable I think is the word actually but then again I am biased! Of course we have lots of other pretty little things like Rosaries and Pendulums; Crystal Balls and Chinese Answer Sticks where you make a wish and shake the holder and as one rises higher than the other you simply read the meaning; it also foretells if your wish will come true also.

Now, another section I have is called 'The Same as it Never Was' due to the fact they are antique or second hand items that I have sourced. The reason I added this section is because all of my personal pieces that I have as décor items are not actually for sale. You can guarantee that each and every day someone tries to purchase them so I figured if I added this section then I can cater for two very different types of clientele? Of course, time is the biggest factor with this section; it takes time to try and find rare individual pieces and sometimes I just don't have time off to go and look. I do love the old pieces though; they carry so much more character than the new pieces. I found a fantastic store where I purchased a trunk, and old luggage trunk that has a stamp with a date posted on there from 1932 in a store called 'Serendipity' right here in Swansea. I fell in love with this store as soon as I walked in there. The trunk has probably seen some amazing places around the world. I also picked up some Antiquarian Books from there and you can just smell the pages as you hold it; it oozes with history and lingering fingers if that makes any sense. You are probably thinking what kind of person get's high on stuff like this? Well, all I have to say is me! I am well and truly the secret 'Geek' of old times past. If I tell you the next story you must believe me. One Saturday Donna Wonna covered the store for me as I was in desperate need of a day off and wanted to spend it with my mum. We decided to go to a place called Rheolla Market about forty minutes away from where we live in Swansea. The reason for going there is because it contains on of the largest Antique stores and Car Boot Sales under one roof and is the perfect little hideaway for hidden treasure; all waiting for me to discover it. I came across a book; it was a Shakespeare book that was published in 1901. I didn't really pay too much attention to the content whilst we were in the Market as there was way too much going on around me that I wanted to explore but when we returned to the car I decided to open it and you will not believe what I found inside it? Who ever owned the book prior to me had placed cuttings of certain flowers inside and listed the page they were to be found on and on one of the pages was 'A FOUR LEAFED CLOVER'. Can you just imagine my excitement?

That very same day, another book I came across was a bible that was dated back to 1899; it was a family owned bible that was passed down to the last person in 1932 on my birthday July 26th. How strange? It's as if both of these items were meant for me. It's truly amazing all of the little things I have found along the way and many items given to me by friends and family members also. A lot of them I raided myself from family members houses and most of them bought specifically but everything has its place and fits in perfectly with the other pieces. It's as if they were waiting for me to go find them, which of course I did. A lot of what I'm speaking about might come across as weird to most but if you have a gift like we do these special items will find you. I have even received signs from the spirits of what stores to go in and where they are located. Signs can come in many different versions from dreams to an article in the newspaper to talking to someone who may mention something you have been searching for but the bottom line is once you 'get' the sign that is being given to you, you just feel it in your heart like nothing you've ever felt before. For those of you who are unsure of what 'The Gift' actually is, let me explain to you because it can come in many different forms. Each and every spiritual person you may meet in your life has something unique of their own but normally it has transpired around some of the following forms; although there are over one hundred ways to help you communicate with the spirit or predict the future; far too many to list but here are some of the most common known to the receiver such as yourself: -

Clairvoyance – 'Clear Seeing' which is when you receive clear images and pictures in your mind from Spirit.

Clairaudience – 'Clear Hearing' which is when you receive clear messages in your head; which sound like your voice but you know are not your thoughts.

Clairsentience – 'Clear Feeling' which is when you experience strong emotional outbursts or smells; you can feel warm or cold as if spirit has brushed up against you.

Clair cognizance – 'Clear Knowing' which 100% feeling of accuracy in predictions through direct flashes or facts being shown before your eyes.

Clairalience – 'Clear Smells' which is where you can smell signs of spirit passed; i.e. cigarette smoke

Clairgustance – 'Clear Taste' which is where you will taste something that spirit is trying to explain to you.

E.S.P – 'Extra Sensory Perception' which is where gifted people know they have access to their sixth sense.

Telepathy – 'Silent Words' which means communicating with someone else through your mind without using words at all.

The more one identifies with what they feel comfortable in practicing with the more successful you become at it, which you will soon learn in the next chapter. One of the biggest things missing in our community at the time of creating the store was hope. I think this was purely down to the recession as so many of the locals lost their jobs and could not find a replacement, which left the moral ever so low. I had an idea of how I could help with this. In my past no matter what position I've held in whatever company I have always emailed a 'Positive Quote of the Day' to every staff member in my team sometimes reaching close to 1000 people as each department head would then forward the quote from within. The location I have chosen to open the store has a very busy passing trade so the creative side of me came out and I have converted one of my store front windows into the 'Positive Quote Window' – powered by Angels! I had Perspex fitted into the window where it hangs from the top to the bottom and has an interchangeable middle where I can go in each and every day and place a new quote. Sometimes I write my own depending on what is going on in my life that day or sometimes I reach out to my favorite books of quotes or search some of my favorite motivational sites on the Internet and use them. Either way what I have chosen to do is most certainly working. You would be absolutely amazed by the amount of people who have actually parked their car in the car park to walk into my store and tell me how they hope they are stuck outside my shop every day to read the quote as it gives them inspiration on a daily basis. That has happened on so many occasions and even the locals that have to pass by get to the corner shop to purchase their morning papers stop to read it. So you see, yet another mission accomplished. I can't put into words the feeling of joy I get in my heart when I receive feedback from people. You see, as much as we all like giving there is no better gift to receive back than gratitude or joy from someone else's happiness and if you think about it, that's how much power each and every one of us has on a daily basis to either make or break someone's day. I chose to make someone's day by giving them wings. It starts with me from the time I write it and I guess it carries on in the next person and the next and the next through a kind deed or simply letting that person in front of you in traffic. It's as easy as that. This was one of the reasons I loved texting them to Derek; I knew if anyone could, he would feel it touch his heart in a way that no one else could, why? Because it was from me that's why. So as you can see all of the pieces of the puzzle were in place to sell and now it's time to take you to what happens behind the shop front walls as we prepare to open…

CHAPTER 16

Take the Lid off the Cauldron!

As you can imagine by now we are pretty excited; exhausted at the same time but I think my adrenaline took over at this stage. No time to eat or to do anything else but just prepare for the big day. Derek kept in contact this whole week to check up on me and whispered the right words that once again kept me going. I truly missed him by now; it was like taking a kid into a candy store and telling them they can have what ever they like but only for a period of time before it's all taken away from you again? I knew I had bigger fish to fry but I just wished he was around to see my project; after all, I was so extremely proud of it. I know I've opened many business's around the world for other companies but there was always a security blanket with them, this time I was it and if I screwed up then it was on my shoulders. Only I could pick up the pieces so I guess of course I'm going to second guess my decisions but I have to say, no more than I did working for any of the other companies. I always treated them as if it was my own and I guess it showed in my delivery of the projects also. The day we opened was manic; we were still dealing with last minute hitches but I have to say it all went extremely well and as much as I was stressed it was worth every hour of lost sleep the night before. Here I am, stood in my own little kingdom just waiting to climb the success tree and I LOVE IT! I don't think I came down off my high that night at all. My phone kept ringing off the hook with people wishing us good luck and so many friends and family came in to give us 'good-luck' cards, I was quite overwhelmed at the support if I'm honest. Everyone wanted us to succeed, even more so because I'd made such a huge transition home from the only life I knew for the past 20 years. I just remember seeing my parent's faces; they were so unbelievably proud. Dad was grinning like a Cheshire cat and mum just had that look on her face as she often did to say 'you've done it again baby, well done'. Mum really has been through the run of the mill with me and each role I've had over the years. Every time I gained promotion or took on another role I would call her in tears claiming I was never going to be able to get a handle on it? Can you believe that?

I've never failed at a role in my entire life and she knew that but she would always be there on the other end of the phone and listen to my tears. Once I stopped she would laugh and say 'we'll have this conversation again in a few months time to see if you still feel the same and rightly so, I wouldn't. I would have most certainly settled in the role by then and be absolutely as high as kite on motivation as per usual! Mum also knew this was different; I'd made a drastic change in my life and everything was riding on it. One of the main features I have in my store in the guest waiting area is a comment book that allows my clients and visitors alike the opportunity to share their views on the store and the reading they received with me. Personally I love this book. If a new client walks in through the door and asks if my readings are any good I just forward them to this area, ask them kindly to read the comments and then allow them to decide for themselves. Guaranteed I will get one or more bookings from the parties in question afterwards. My parents of course had to be one of the first comments in the book and again as they should be. As usual Dad gets fed up after ten minutes and so they left. The girls hung around for a little while and then we left that night and went to Bingo of all places to celebrate my birthday, can you believe that? I am very proud to say that we opened without any glitches what so ever! Everything went to plan and as happy as I was I just needed a glass of wine! To launch the business I placed a half page article inside the local paper called 'The South Wales Evening Post'. The article was wonderful; it included the family history and practically everything anyone needed to know about the store and what we offered. My phone was off the hook with calls, in the end I carried the appointment book around with me for fear of losing clients but literally I was completely booked for the first 5-6months. Your probably wondering what was I booked with? My gift is the gift of Tarot Cards. I was given my very first pack when I was nineteen years of age and have practiced with them ever since. Tarot has to be one of the most difficult things to learn as there are so many of them but the scary thing about them is that they are never wrong and that is from a please or offend stand point. Shiv gave me my cards as a leaving present when I first moved away to work on ships and I guess I haven't been able to part with them. I do believe that once you feel your niche with something you should try and nurture it.

For years I searched for a Crystal Ball; just like Nanna O'Conner and couldn't seem to find one anywhere. All the countries I traveled to and I just couldn't find one. I know to some that might sound strange but again not to me. I guess I was just not meant to use that tool to channel my gift; I was meant to use the Tarot that was given to me and so I did. For years and years I practiced on family members and on myself and I really did have a knack as they say. My timing has sometimes proven to be wrong but my cards are always right. I loved working with them, even though they were quite difficult to begin with but the more I used them the more it became like second nature. So when we opened the store we offered Tarot Card Readings and I was pretty much booked up between 5-10 clients a day. Donna would take the overflow. Some days it would be quiet but for the most part it was steady.

Since the store has opened it has turned into a wonderful almost magical place. One morning going back last October, my routine would be to place the Sandwich board outside with our telephone number posted on it, open the curtains, light the incense sticks, turn on the music, change the positive quote of the day in the window, turn on the lamps in my private reading room, check the phone for voice mails and most importantly wish everyone and everything in my store a 'Good Morning'. I would even say it to the spirits. This was the same ritual at night when I closed, there wasn't one day that went by that I would leave without thanking the Universe for my day and wish everyone a 'Goodnight'. Over the following few months I would notice that things had been moved and I would find things on the floor that weren't there the night before I left? I was convinced my store has come to life. I always knew that the items I'd purchased were for a reason but I had no idea what I was about to experience. You have to understand something here; I wasn't sure if what I was beginning to see and hear was the spirits playing with me or if it really was happening but please bare with me because it's taken me a while to come to terms with this but now that I have it is SO MUCH FUN! All of a sudden I was becoming more aware of my surroundings and everything in it. Each day I would open up and not know what to expect. I would find sweets on the shelves and ornaments had been moved, the music would be on and the one thing that completely freaked me out but in a nice way was I would find feathers. Everyone on this planet knows that if you are lucky enough to find a feather then that simply means one thing, you are being watched over by the Divine Angels themselves.

I can't say I was surprised by that really, after all they are the ones who went out of their way to give me the signs about moving back to Wales. Why would I be shocked they are looking out for me here? So the more I felt comfortable with what I was seeing the more they felt comfortable in opening up to me. It was as if I was in a different world. They? Who are they? They are the most wonderful little things that come to life when no one is watching! There are some things that don't sleep or should I say unless they pretend they are sleeping to that I can't annoy them! Let me introduce you to my magical little friends. We'll start out with the story of the Lucky Leprechaun. Going back to June last year a friend of mine was going to Ireland for a few days on a conference with work and I had asked him to pick me up a Leprechaun for luck for my store, only he forgot! How can anyone possibly forget to pick up a Leprechaun if you're in Ireland? They must be all over the place I'm sure but that's fine and that's men for you. Then a few months ago a very dear friend of my sister Donna asked us if we would like a box of old trinket's from her Grandfather's house after he passed away? Well, we never say no to merchandise that could possibly have a great history value than the $$$. Over to the store comes this box and lo and behold inside was none other than a 'Lucky Leprechaun'. You see, it was meant to find a way inside my shop and this little guy sits on the edge of my cash register. One morning I could have sworn I saw him wink at a client as she walked up to my reception desk to schedule an appointment because his eye almost twinkled like a star at night! Now of course my immediate reaction was perhaps it was just the sun shining through the window and caught the reflection of something but when I stopped to look at it I seriously thought I was going nuts. I must say, it did scare me for almost a few seconds but I have no idea why because another amazing part of my gift is that I speak to the spirits, I talk to dead people! What can be scarier than that right? Over the next few days I kept my eyes on the cheeky little chappy, I was convinced I was going to catch him out when he wasn't looking but I never did. Days passed by and for some reason, I would be sat in the store and never felt as if I was alone. I know I had the spirits with me but that was always a different feeling than what I was experiencing now. I felt as if there was something special being hidden from me and take my word for it I was determined to get to the bottom of it!

Playing Miss Marple the detective I decided I would plant certain things around the shop to see if anything would happen to them when I returned the next day and right enough it had. I tried not to show my surprise as I saw things I wanted to act as if it was 'the norm' for me. Most importantly if what was happening was what I think was happening I needed to be very careful in my approach to ensure that I wouldn't spook the other parties so to speak. Curious? I'm sure you are but I think it's time to come clean with you. At the finish of every day I would always leave out the back door entrance of the store, as it was closest to the alarm so that I could simply run out the door. One night I had a plan, I would pretend to push the alarm buttons and only to my knowledge I canceled it out also so I was actually closing the store without the alarm being set. I can hear everyone's curiosity here asking why on earth would I do that right? O.K, here's why. I walked upstairs to the apartment, changed my clothes and took Sooty out for a walk. After we returned I sneaked down the back stairs as quietly as I could and opened up the back door of the store. In between the back door and the shop is a fire door; which also keeps out any sounds. I placed my ear to the door and could hear music, laughter and fluttering sounds as if something was flying around the room? I opened the door and to my shock, surprise and overwhelming sense of excitement I was right, everything came to life. The ornaments, the gifts, everything! I don't know who was shocked more, them or me but they seemed more scared than I was and that was the last thing I wanted. I had to think fast on my feet here before they froze back to normal but I'm not the most diplomatic person on the planet and all that I could think of was 'I gotcha'. What? Talk about freak them out even more, which would never have worked. As soon as I realized what I'd said I tried to redeem myself and spoke a load of rubbish. They all just stopped and stared at me; I think they expected me to scream or something and then one of the fairies that was flying came up close to my face and said 'Can you see us, really'? Of course I could see them and I was bursting with joy at the fact I wasn't actually dreaming. I wanted them to calm down though because all I could hear was panic, they were all trying to find their way back to their positions and of course kept banging into each other until in the end I shouted 'Stop'. There was silence for a few seconds and then all of a sudden one of the 'Witch' ornaments that was the image of me in my Halloween costume came forward and said hello. I asked what her name was and she said 'Angie', she explained that she was made as a replica of me to reassure me and she would always protect my gift to assist with my questioning mind. The very strange thing about this is that she actually sounded like me also? I was freaked out, her hair color, eyes, nose and skin coloring was the same only her gown was glistening in a deep copper color, not white like mine. She did speak a lot softer than I do so I did have to pay close attention to what she was saying. This side of her was most certainly not like me, the only time I'm quiet is when I'm sleeping! Mini me managed to calm everyone down and after she did I asked her to introduce me to everyone. The first person to jump in the front of the line was none other than 'The Lucky Leprechaun'. He was ever such a gentleman and actually took off his hat as he introduced himself to me. The Lucky Leprechaun would stand there looking at his watch to see what time I would open up and if I was early he'd pretend to faint and if I was late he would tut his mouth. God forbid if I forgot something during the set up, I wouldn't live it down he would say 'If you were Irish you wouldn't forget'. Well I'm not bloody Irish and I am the only person here so if I forget it comes to me sooner or later.

Now, the next person I would like you to meet is the sweet fairy. My store is located just around the corner from one of the local schools so each and every day the kids would pop in and make a wish in the wishing well or simply wander around the store in awe of it's contents. Of course they would hover over the sweets. Now, Penny the sweet fairy is absolutely stunning. She is sitting down with her knees bent and her arms wrapped around her knees. She is actually sitting on a pond leaf and the leaf curves up to create a dish where of course the sweets sit. Now if there is a child that would like a sweet and has been good that day in school then she would wink at them and allow them to take one but if the child has been naughty that day then she will simply slap their hand with one of her wings and won't allow them to take a sweet! I tried to talk her out of this but she insisted on doing things her way, who am I to tell her any different? I'm just the store owner right? Believe it or not it does actually work because the kids who were naughty the day before would walk back into the store with great excitement after being good in school that day and run over to Penny to see if she would allow them to have a sweet. Of course none of the parents could see this, these secrets were only visible to the children unless the adults were themselves either still 'young at heart' or they had to be a 100%

believer. Penny was so graceful; she would sit there and barely say a word to a soul, even me? She would smile at me and just watch with a smile on her face as the people would come and go from the store. As an ornament she has a tear just underneath her left eye but as soon as she is awake to the world the tears disappear. After many attempts of asking where the tear came from she explained that she had lost her family not long after being shipped to Wales. They were meant to be a set that would all stay together but the lady who owned them got offered to make some serious money if she sold them separately and so she did. So you see, we are now Penny's family and this is why her tears stop when she's surrounded by us. Penny thought for the longest time that she would never be able to talk again and was ever so lonely sitting in a box waiting to be sold but she always kept hope that one day she would be with friends that loved her again. We love her very much and are so thankful she ended up with us. Over to the left of Penny is an Egyptian Cat. This was a gift from my Dad for the store to bring me luck only as you know Cats are the most elegant things and snobby so he does tend to keep himself to himself sitting on the top shelf all regal with his diamante's all over the podium that he's sat on. He is a sandy color cat with very distinctive black markings. He would always give me a heads up on my parents. You see I nick named them 'The Wrinklies' because when they came out to see me in Miami they wanted to be in bed by 9pm every night! They earned the title let me tell you, so as soon as they pull into the car park outside 'Cleo' turns to me and says 'Incoming – The Wrinklies have arrived'. As soon as he does, Mini Me hops on her broomstick and tells everyone to behave! You'd swear it was the royal Family arriving but I guess they are our King and Queen of the Barnett family. My mum and dad always make sure they go out of their way to walk around the store and say hello to everyone, after all it is their home and they just feel its imperative that they know how appreciative they are that everyone in my store look after me. You see I'll always be the baby no matter what age I am. Of course as usual Dad always gets fed up easily and wants to leave five minutes after he's arrived so mum does tend to come on her own a lot of the time, that way she can wander around the store and always ends up spending money on a gift for everybody else, never for herself!

Now the biggest attraction of my store has to be the 'Wishing Well'. People get off buses and walk into my store just to make a wish in the well. The kids absolutely adore the idea of this and most of them come in almost every day to make a wish. All of the proceeds to the well get emptied once a year and are donated to 'The Cynthia Barnett Think Pink Charity Fund'; this year we donated £122.00. I was delighted to take these coins that were empowered by someone's wish and then passed back to help someone else in need? What a fantastic thought right? Let me share something about the well though, not everyone who enters the store is eligible to make a wish. The key ingredient needed is belief. If someone who doesn't believe that their wish will come true when they throw their coin in the 'Wishing Well' simply spits the coin back out! I was so embarrassed the first time this happened. How can you explain that to a child or to an adult that has so much going on in their world that they have lost all hope of things actually improving in their life? I will say it does make you laugh though because as the coin comes back it also splashes the person who threw it with water! I'm am proud to say that to this day I have never had a coin thrown back to me, thank god. That wouldn't exactly look right would it being the owner and creator of the store and not believing? I have asked it some funky questions to be on the safe side by tricking it with certain questions and I'm taking it that the Wishing

KICK START THE BROOMSTICK

Well must love me because everything I ask for some how seems to come true.

This is a perfect way to introduce my 'Wishing Doll'. This is a Voodoo doll of the nice kind! It is a plain rag doll that you have to dress yourself; it has absolutely no detail on it what so ever. You have to give it eyes, a mouth etc., You also have to sew things to the external part of the doll; whether it be money if you require this or hearts if you are looking for love or happiness etc., The whole kit comes with trinkets that help you design your very own personal doll. My Wishing Doll is situated on the top of one of the book cases in my store on a rocking chair and it freaks everyone out when they come in due to the fact it actually does look like a Voodoo Doll, many people have requested to buy one but do you think I can source them anywhere? I even reached out to the company I purchased mine from in the US to see if they sold wholesale but they had eliminated that product? I couldn't believe it! One of the spooky things about my doll is that when one of my wishes is about to come true she starts rocking and the whole store gets excited about which one of my wishes it will be and they all sit there and chatter about it. My only hope is that she didn't rock when strangers were in the store because I didn't want them to be spooked by it. If she did I would try my hardest to take them away from that bookshelf to prevent any questions. Sometimes I would be too late and they would ask if I saw her rock? Of course I would lie but I have to tell you though, I did love it; as soon as I saw it rocking my heart would just skip a beat and I would say out loud 'Thank You' to the Universe again because I had faith that once again my prayers were being answered, maybe not in the order of how I requested them but they were coming to fruition all at the same time.

One of the funniest things about everything coming to life was the

'Money Plants'. Of course they don't have faces so would make the strangest noises as they shook with laughter. They used to threaten to stop the phone from ringing if I didn't water them! Of course I have the plants all over the store so you could do nothing but laugh at these plants; the more you laughed the more they would shake, you almost wanted to do a little jig with them but I couldn't afford to have the phone stop ringing so I would water them almost every other day and make sure they got plenty of sunlight. The weird thing about these plants is that you will always find a money spider spinning a web on them. You know what money spiders look like right? They are the tiny little black ones that you are supposed to let them run across your palm, that means money is expected to come to you from a source. I always let them run until they hop off, only when they do you can never find them again because they are so small. You remember me telling you about the prayer and protection bracelets right? Well, the most amazing thing happens with these in the store. I always tell people to feel for the one they want to purchase but now what happens is the bracelet that's meant for the person buying it will rise above the others, float and almost illuminate until the person chooses it. When customers leave the shop all of the saints actually talk to each other and oh boy what a racket it is! All you can hear them saying to each other is 'So, do you know what I'm famous for?' and they will literally tell each other their stories; it's interesting actually because I've learned so much from them that I probably wouldn't have before but the funny thing is they do it every day! You'd swear it is the first time they've spoken to each other because they are so passionate about how they actually introduce themselves. I just smile and pretend I'm busy so that I don't have to get involved in the conversation!

When you come into the store, behind the reception desk on the wall you will see a huge collage of family memorabilia that contains everything from Seaman's Certificates that were issued to my great grandfather dated back to the 1800's. There is a stamp in there that is also worth over one hundred pounds it's that old. There are wedding certificates that are from 1832 also; it's amazing to look at. My grandmother kept all sorts of things like this but the great thing about this is that when you stood in front of collage it would introduce you to the person it represented and tell you about their life, their loves and bring you to the connection of the present day family member. This is like the Wikipedia of the family; you can ask it as many questions as you like and it will answer them. If you are a family member trying to read the documents they will tell you how you are connected to them and from which family member; it truly is pretty cool actually. There is such a lovely photo of both my Auntie Rosie and My Auntie Popo. Popo is only a little girl and is so very pretty. Believe it or not, all of the documents that are in there came from my Nanna Forester's house thanks to Auntie Popo. I asked Popo if I could use them when I first opened the store. I couldn't believe it when I went through the old boxes; I was simply in awe. I felt like I was in 'Antique Heaven'.

I left with more than just documents that day; I also managed to take with me old medicine bottles and creams dating from the early 1900's. I can't believe my Nanna would keep things like that, it's as if she knew one day they would come in very handy isn't it? They are all such great conversation starters and you would be amazed at how many people try to buy them from me. I have promised Popo I would look after them and never part with them. One of the really exciting things she gave me on loan was the replica car toy of 'Chitty Chitty Bang Bang'. The only thing about this car is it is missing one of the girls from the back seat. My grandfather worked in Met toys Factory for years and this was actually a collector's piece. Met toys were the largest supplier of toys in the country at the time and it seems as if everyone I knew from that generation worked there at some point or another. Not quite sure what happened to them though? There was one item that I wasn't allowed to leave with and that was the family bible. Oh my goodness; you should see this bible it is amazing. Apparently it has been in the family for generations and it truly looks and smells like it also. Inside you will find flower cuttings and cards that were written and placed at people's funerals, family members of course. The ribbons that were wrapped around the flowers still had the mud on them today. It's amazing really isn't it? It almost makes me want to create a blast from my past for someone to open it and read it one day and think and feel the same as I did the day I went through all of my family's belongings. I was so happy to have something of my Nanna's in the store; after all she wasn't around to see any of it although I will say I know she is around me at times because I can smell her scent, not her perfume but her actual scent. You would have loved my Nanna Forester; she was such an amazing woman. She was ever so much the lady but believe it or not she did have such a funny sense of humor. The one thing about Nanna Forester was if you told her you loved her she would say 'and you'. She would never come out and say it back. Funny really because she never had to actually say the words; you would just know exactly what she was trying to say either by her voice or by the look in her eye. She was ever such a kind and gentle person.

At the store we also have greeting cards for sale that have everything from Angels to witches to Buddha's and dragons on the front of them. If you catch them on a good day they will talk to you and let you know what kind of person they would be suitable for. They are the cutest things on the planet because they are also very respectable to the other cards surrounding them so if they think there is a more suitable card in the rack they will tell you but be prepared to be asked questions, they will want to know the ins and outs of the person you are buying for because to them it has to be perfect and believe it or not they are always right. The amount of times people have come back into the store to say 'thank you', because the card they chose was perfect is quite astonishing but more so rewarding. Even the cards feel like they deserve a pat on the back when that happens. So as you can see my store truly has come to life. Everything in it has its very own special personality. The funny side to this is they would play games with me. If there was a CD playing that they didn't like then they would simply turn if off. It would be quite frustrating for me, especially when I was in the middle of a reading but they knew I was thinking the exact same thing. It was time to change the music.

Over the next few months I became very connected to everything in my store and I have to say they became very protective of me also. From the time I opened my door in the morning to the time I left at night I felt protected. So much so that in my private reading room I had several ornaments that also became very special to me. I have a hand that explains all of the lines and what each one means so if you were to have a palm reading done it would help you to understand. This ornament always reminds me of the Adams Family because just like the hand in that movie where it would answer the phone mine would simply tap me on the shoulder to let me know if someone came into the store. You see, I have the most wonderful person working with me but she only works when I am booked solidly with clients. If I only have a few clients a day then I will work the floor and keep an eye out on the shop in between clients. It doesn't affect my readings because I simply pick up from where I left off. I used to have someone that worked for me in the past but to be perfectly honest with you she was so lazy. I remember one time I asked her to do something; she was reading a book at the time. She asked me 'can I finish my chapter first'? I nearly fell through the floor, how cheeky was that right? She had more balls than the world cup to say a comment like that to your boss!

My private reading room was a wonderful place to be in. If you remember me telling you about the photo shoot I did for the collateral, well I have my Angel wings hanging in my room and whenever I do a reading for someone, if a spirit comes through to try and communicate with the person I'm reading for then the feathers on my Angel wings start to flutter. It was strange at first for me to come to terms with this but I knew instantly when this happened that there was a message from someone waiting for me to tell the person I was reading for. I want you to understand something about my gift and me. Even though my Nanna O'Conner always told us 'It is the living you need to be afraid of, not the dead' I was still pretty freaked out at the thought of seeing spirits. For years I had heard them but didn't know how I would react if I saw them and so I asked them not to show themselves to me. That was until my brother passed away. I can't say I was scared of them, after all they'd given me so much joy over the last how many years its just that I never thought I would want to see them, until now. More than ever I wanted to see them. I begged and begged for them to show themselves to me but they haven't. I guess I don't have the choice? I have to wait until they are ready to show themselves to me. It is frustrating though; it would make things so much easier to pass on wonderful messages.

Donna Wonna went to a car boot sale one day and found the most amazing witch. She had a sensor embedded in her that as soon as someone walked by her she would talk. Well let me tell you about

KICK START THE BROOMSTICK

'Witchy Lou'. She was like the mother of the store. Each and every morning I would walk in she would be stood there, arms crossed waiting to tell me what mischief everyone had got up to the night before. The hilarious part about this is that the Three Australian Witches that were given to me as gifts would protect her and defend her to the high heavens. I would be subjected to listening to all of the shenanigans that everyone had been up to over night; especially if it was the weekend when I finally decided to take the day off. Everyone in the store could not believe what a 'clecker' she was; she would spill the beans on absolutely everything. Of course I would listen but I would not pay too much attention to it; after all I think she was just getting old, as sad as that sounds. The kids love her though, they all want to play with her when they come into the store and because she actually moves her mouth as she talks it's quite spooky really at how human the plastic features actually look. Every night before I leave the store I ask her to look after everyone for me until the next day; she likes to think she is the boss and this makes her feel special. One thing she can't stand though is when children under the age of five come in and start squeezing her nose and pulling her hair, she just gives me the look as if to say 'are you going to let them get away with this'? Of course as soon as they leave she dusts off her dress, puts her hair straight and mumbles 'The Wicked Witch from the West in the Wizard of Oz didn't have to put up with this', and I reply with 'no, but your still alive and she isn't'.

CHAPTER 17

Unwanted Energy!

Since the store has opened I have experienced some very strange things. I was told many years back that I would be involved with rescue work. What that means is that spirits who have issues with passing over to the other side whether it be because of committing suicide or simply being lost and cant seem to find the light, they need help to cross over. I never imagined in my wildest dreams did I ever see myself doing something like this but believe it or not I've had to help two gentleman pass over. Both were suicide cases and without going too much into detail they couldn't go unless messages were passed to their family members and this is where I would come into the equation. I would be the person to pass on the message to their family members during their reading with me. Sometimes it's difficult to approach the situation, especially if the family members are still upset with the fact they took their own lives. This makes it harder for them to communicate with me. On more than one occasion a spirit has actually attached itself to me and won't leave me. How do I know? I feel the most horrendous heavy dizzy feeling and am absolutely drained of all energy. It's a very uncomfortable but strange feeling but each time it happens it hits me it's like a ton of bricks and the only way I can get rid of them is to completely cleanse myself and my room, put myself to bed and sleep it off. There has been a situation where I had to get the help of my sister's as the energy of one man was way to strong for me to handle on my own. The one time that sticks out the most is every now and again friends and family will bring me things that they think I might like for the store. One of the girls gave us a box of things from her grandfather's house after he passed away. I can't explain how I know this but something wasn't right in my store after they arrived. I kept getting the feeling that something or someone was angry all the time and the negative energy was keeping people away from my store. I tried my hardest to ask it to leave but to no avail; which made me realize it had to be connected to one of the ornaments? Donna came down to do a reading for me in the store and so I asked her to walk around and see if she could pick up on what it was? I think I was too close to the problem being here every day and I'm not sure I would have been able to detect this. Donna walked in every corner of the shop and came across a Toby Jug of King Henry VIII; she took one look at it and had goose bumps the size of golf balls! This was the culprit? I didn't understand at first but as we all know he was a dictator and therefore was trying to take over the positive energy of the store. I picked it up and placed it inside a carrier bag and threw it out.

Donna could hear him saying the most horrendous things to her and his language was foul apparently which didn't scare her but it did make her realize she was right. As soon as it left my store the room became brighter and a lot warmer than you can ever imagine. Whenever anything like this happened or someone from the street came in and left a negative energy behind the three brooms on the wall, one that belonged to each of us three girls would fly on their own and start from the center of the shop and sweep the energy out the door. It was amazing to see, they would be the first ones on the case, often before I could even ask for their help and they would simply sweep the negativity right out the door and everyone in the store would cheer once they were finished but just don't get in their way or you'll end up on your backside on the pavement outside; which has happened on more than one occasion and it's hilarious to watch. Talk about a traffic stopper; all the cars go by and beep their horns because some of the locals are all familiar with this now.

I absolutely loved everything that was happening in the store and wish I would have told the world about it but I couldn't. Not everyone takes lightly to this kind of thing. There are some serious skeptics out there but there are also the serious believers. I've never tried to push my beliefs of anyone or tried to convert them into my way of thinking but if they ask for stories then I will take great pride in sharing some of mine. Naturally it's hard not to believe after hearing them but like I said the choice is theirs. I used to be quite scared of people thinking I was a bit of a nut job at first but at the end of the day I know I'm not. I wouldn't describe myself as normal but what is normal today? I don't profess to be normal but I do know that there is very little wrong with me. I have scared off a few potential men in the past though; especially when I was in the states. I had to be very careful when choosing who I could truly open up too. I'm not going to hide who I am because of the gift I have. Doing this for a living does not make me any lesser a person than the next corporate big wig does it? Derek on the other hand remembers what it was like in my grandmother's house when we were kids and so it does make it easier for me with him although I'm not convinced to this day he would feel comfortable in introducing me to his friends but that doesn't bother me. I will say that he has shown a lot more interest in it when we've spent time together and has asked lots of different questions about it, which I was surprised at? It was quite nice for a change to see him so intrigued. We didn't really have much time together when we saw each other and so we would try and fit in as many questions and cover as many topics as we could in that space of time. I have no idea when it comes to his line of work so we are equal.

Not all men are skeptics though. Believe it or not, since my store has opened 40% of my clients are male and here's the surprising factor to that, the majority of them are business men looking for guidance and confirmation on business deals that they are working on and I will say that out of all of the men that come to me I have managed to retain 90% of them due to the results they've received from their readings. I have some male clients that come to me once a month for readings and some that come once a week. Generally speaking it's the men that are sometimes embarrassed to tell people they come for guidance but they love to see the results; they get high on it. You would be absolutely amazed at how many different types of people that enter my store for either a reading or simply to pick up items to practice with. The great thing about what we do is that there is absolutely no demographic for this store; I have clients as young as sixteen and I think the eldest person I have read for was eighty-two and she was looking for love so it just goes to show you that you never give up on things no matter what age? I don't really like reading for anyone younger than sixteen and therefore I refuse too basically. In my eyes they haven't really lived yet and are so very vulnerable to every piece of information you give them and so can often live by what you tell them; which is not healthy. They need to use their own free will at this stage in their life or will live to almost regret it. Most teenagers don't know what they want out of life at that age and I don't mean to be condescending when I say that it's just that I remember how I was, I didn't have a clue of what I wanted to do when I left school and so I became a sheep and followed my friends into a career that would open many doors for me but one I would absolutely

Unwanted Energy

end up hating! I have read for one person who was under sixteen but that was because his mum thought he had a negative energy attached to him, which turned out to be him being lazy basically and didn't really have the motivation to want to help himself.

It was quite sad but there was only so much someone like myself can do to help him without him wanting to help himself. It's amazing what the kinds of issues people have and why they consult with the occult. Whenever I sit for someone to do a Tarot Reading I always ask them a bunch of questions, firstly to find out how they heard about us to give me an idea of where my marketing dollars are being spent and secondly to see if they have come for a specific reason. Most people are hesitant in telling you why they've come in hopes that I can pick up on it; which 99% of the time I do but sometimes it can be quite difficult, especially if they are hard to read for and so I always ask them at the end if there is anything else they would like answers with. It's very important for me that my clients leave happy, after all word of mouth is the best form of advertising and so when they leave I want them to leave with a positive attitude and more importantly I want them to leave with hope. Hope that what they have been told during their reading will in actual fact come true. The only time people leave my room unhappy is if they are told something they either don't want to hear or if they are told that their life is not currently going to change dramatically? I absolutely love my Tarot Cards. They were given to me at 19 years of age and I have looked after them very well. The great thing about them is if they need to be cleaned or if there is any negative energy lingering in my room on any of the cards they will tell me. Every card comes to life. How it works with me is I lay my cards out in a fan shape on the table in my room and I get my clients to choose the cards they want. They have to really feel for the right card to come to them whether it is through the heat of the cards or by a tingling sensation but the majority of the time it is on pure gut instinct. I will always advise them that they will not choose the wrong cards; that's the amazing thing about Tarot, they choose you. Another thing I always tell the person I am reading for is I will only tell them the truth and that is whether it is from a please or offend standpoint. One thing I am actually quite proud to say is that my timing may sometimes be off with my predictions due to the fact there is no timing in the spirit world but my cards are never wrong. There has been once or twice that my clients have left my room upset with either what I've told them or don't believe what I tell them or don't have any communication with the spirits of their choice; which I'll explain more now in detail. Watch this space will be my only response.

The amount of people that have come back to tell me that what I've told them has actually come true is beyond me. You can guarantee that probably 2-3 clients per week will go out of their way to either call me on the phone or actually pop into the store. I of course can't say I'm shocked, without sounding too cocky but I absolutely love the success stories. Sometimes it may take a little longer than anticipated but I find it extremely rewarding; especially if someone has just been told that there is a pregnancy for them or a new relationship for someone that is so unbelievably lonely with their life or if someone is about to land that perfect job. I LOVE MY JOB!!!! The results are the best thank you I could possibly wish to receive.

Of course those three topics are probably in the top ten of things most of my clients want answers with; the most obvious is money. My Tarot Cards could tell a fair few juicy stories though and probably get me hung in the meantime. It's interesting actually because you would be amazed at how much goes on in peoples lives; it almost makes mine look boring! I have been faced with everything from love triangles to married people turning gay and their husband/wife doesn't know. To drug addictions; sex addictions; business scams; family scams and arguments etc. You name it and I've probably heard it. As soon as the client I'm reading for has chosen the cards, I lay them out in a way only I understand aside from the cards themselves. Once all the cards turn over they get ever so excited; especially if there is some juiciness going on and always want to go first but of course I calm them down and follow the order that the spirits give me. The client may not be able to resonate with anything I am saying at the time but I always tell them to write things down because without a doubt things will unfold at some point over the timeframe we've given them. It's always good to look back on also, I do that often with readings I've actually had in the past. My cards are pretty cool in the way they work from a timing standpoint. If I get three or four of the same number in my spread I get so excited! I'm nut's I swear but when this happens I am very seldom wrong. The great thing about my cards is that we have now built a great working relationship with each other and if there is a message I sometimes don't see or miss for whatever strange reason then they will continue to show themselves to me or jump out of the pack until I notice them. Either way my cards won't let my clients leave until they have been given every bit of information possible. This again is vital for me; the more information they leave with the better chance they have of more things happening for them. One of the things I will say is that if after my clients have had their reading and certain things haven't come true then there is a possible chance that their destiny might have altered along the way. They might not have done this themselves but it may have been altered for someone who is connected to their reading; which in turn ultimately affects all involved. Believe it or not I see this a lot; but on this note I must remind you that unfortunately my cards are guidance tools and therefore should only be used as that. Don't take everything literally and you will be surprised by what you will get out of it. The Universe can make things change for you on a daily basis. A lot of this has to do with your thoughts and feelings that you put out there. You know the saying be careful what you wish for because it might just come true? I am living proof of that; I seriously thought I would lose my job with the first company I worked for in Miami and I did. I'd thought about moving home and I did. I'd thought about opening my own business and I did and last but not least I'd thought about Derek coming back into my life and he did. For how long no one knew but all I know is that he is back for now and I am simply loving it.

Back to the readings. One of the most wonderful gifts we have as a family is that we speak to spirits. This has taken years of practice for me to come to terms with. Since childhood I could hear strange things but didn't truly understand how to handle it? My first real experience was actually quite scary. I remember it well. I was nineteen years of age at the time and working on my first cruise ship. We had all been ashore for the day in Venezuela and had a wonderful time. It was my day off this day and so I had showered after getting back on board and decided to have an afternoon siesta. I remember waking up and not being able to breath or move my right side of my body, it was as if someone was sitting on my chest and this probably lasted about ten seconds; although it probably felt like a lifetime to me. As this weight lifted I could hear a very angry mans voice saying negative horrible things to me and as soon as it lifted I dived out of bed and ran into the corridor to see if anyone was around. As I reached the steps leading to the next corridor I sat there and thought 'how can I possibly explain this to someone, they'll either think I've just experienced a nightmare or I have seriously lost my marbles'.

Unwanted Energy

I chose to sit there in silence and take it all in. Now what I haven't shared with you yet is the fact that two nights prior to experiencing this we had decided to conduct the Ouija Board in my cabin. My Nanna O'Conner would have gone ballistic with me if she knew, she always warned us from playing with fire and to her this was the one of the worst things you could do to get burnt. I guess we were all just curious at the time? We just wanted to dabble and one of the girls had some serious questions she needed answers with and didn't feel my Tarot Cards at the time would help her somehow so there were about four or five of us if my memory serves me correctly all on the floor in my cabin. You have to bare in mind that the cabins were ultra small with a set of bunk beds in them, two single wardrobes and a dressing table with a mirror so we had no choice but to use the floor. At the time I don't think any of us truly did believe what was happening and we were convinced that one of the girls was moving the glass. We created all of the letters from paper so it was actually more powerful due to the fact it had our energies all over them but we didn't know that at the time. The glass started wobbling and moving around, not really giving us anything specific and then when we all took our fingers off it, it moved on its own and smashed into the wall of the cabin. Of course some of the girls were in shock and ran out the door screaming and me and another girl Debbie were left sat there to pick up the glass, only we seriously needed to decide what to do with it? We didn't want any of the energies to be lingering in my cabin or on us so we took the letters and the broken glass up to the crew deck of the ship and decided after burning the letters we would throw everything overboard. There was absolutely no way on this planet did we expect any energy to be lingering in my cabin and so I made Debbie stay with me that night after my experience earlier on in the day and I made sure I asked for the good spirits and the Angels to protect me from that moment on. Over the next few days we did hear some weird things in the cabin and things would move around on their own. My cabin mate Christine was convinced that there was still something around, which stopped her sleeping in the cabin. She made great friends with James who was the pianist in one of the lounges at the time. James was gay but they became the best of friends and did everything together. Christine was a bit of a wild card. I think she'd lived a crazy life before joining the ships with me but one the strangest things I remember about her is that everything smelt of mildew with her, her clothes, her make-up, practically everything? Now with this smell coming off all of her things it was bound to affect my things and me? I bought so many air freshener's at the time trying to spruce up the room but thankfully she didn't last the whole contract, she resigned something like 4 months into it? Christine was a lovely person though and it would be interesting to see what happened to her over the years. We never stayed in contact unfortunately. I think the biggest experience I had that left the most impact on me was when I was twenty years of age, still on ships on I was mid way through one of the world cruises and we were in Japan. I had gone out for the day shopping with friends and kept hearing strange voices all the time only I wasn't sure of where they were coming from. I asked the girls at the time if they could hear them also but of course they couldn't? Throughout the day the voices became so loud and so oppressive I decided to get in a cab and head back to the ship; which was really scary actually. I didn't speak Japanese and they didn't speak English so I had a map on my lap of the port where we were docked and gave it to the driver and told him to take me there.I decided to go straight back to my cabin to lye down. My head was absolutely pounding through what I was experiencing. I remember resting for a little while but then we had dinner plans in Kobe that night and I needed to get ready. As I was about to leave my cabin I opened the door and all of a sudden the voices became clear and I could hear everything they were trying to tell me and they said 'be careful, be careful, be careful'? I stopped to think about what I was hearing and for the life of me couldn't understand what they meant. As I opened the cabin door to leave the voices just got stronger and stronger in my head and so I locked the door and turned to walk down the corridor. What I didn't see was as I started walking was a huge puddle of water on the floor that I slipped on. I went up in the air and landed on my ankle that was diagnosed afterwards as being dislocated. As soon as I fell the voices disappeared. It was as if they were trying to warn me about the water but of course due to the fact this was my first experience I didn't understand how to listen to them or what to look out for after receiving them. I was completely spooked by this and was actually quite scared. I took myself off to see the doctor to sure I was O.K. and able to get off the ship. I just knew I had to call home and I just knew I needed to get Nanna's help with this. By the time I managed to hobble off the ship I felt really sorry for myself and was in hysterics crying. I called my mum first and with the time difference is was quite late but they expected late calls due to the schedule I was on at the time. Mum picked up the phone and all she could hear was me sobbing on the other end, she immediately panicked as you can imagine but once I told her what had happened her reaction was simply fantastic and she said 'we all knew this day was going to come but I just wish I was with you to help you through it'. I love my mum so much; she always knows what to say to calm me down. After giving her all of the details she demanded I call Nanna O'Conner to tell her what had happened and to get some guidance from her spirits on how to ensure I am protected from any negative energy coming through. By the time I got off the phone from mum it was quite late but she told me it was best that she call Nanna first to give her a heads up so that she could expect my call.

The phone rang for only a few seconds and as soon as I heard her voice I once again burst into tears. At first she almost chuckled slightly to see my reaction to what had happened. She then explained to me that my first experience was very similar to her own but only I needed to be strong now, not just for myself and for the spirits because if they were aware of how upset I was she was afraid they wouldn't try and come back so I almost had to pretend that I was comfortable with everything that had happened. Just hearing Nanna speak immediately made me feel a sense of calm and as much as I was trying too but it was so hard to get my words out through crying she instantly knew what I was trying to say and that was how unbelievably excited she was that my day had finally come and that she always told me it would but now what? Nanna wanted to make sure I hadn't picked any energy up in the mean time and so she told me that she would be sending the spirits from her house to look after me and make sure I would be O.K. Oh my goodness; Nanna had never done this for anyone before and I felt like I had just grown wings? Her very own personal spirits to look after me? I felt so very honored and cant even begin to tell you how protected I felt. The interesting part of this is that I could tell you exactly the moment they arrived. I had just hung up the phone from her and was heading back to the ship. I reached my cabin, crutches in tow and as I went to open the door I felt a draft appear from nowhere that softly touched the skin on my hands and face with the most amazing smell of my Nanna's perfume. I welcomed them into my cabin and told them how thankful I was for them to be around me and I hoped they would stay until my heart told them I no longer needed them. Nanna's spirits stayed with me for three days and three nights, the power of three comes to life again and just as softly as they came, they left. The next few years I have to say were not only some of the most interesting times but somewhat challenging with regards to my gift. It took me a very long time to learn how switch it on and off when I wanted too. You see, for those reading this who actually do practice the gift you will understand where I am coming from when I say that the spirits if not controlled will try and come through at any given moment or chance they get. I would be in the strangest of places, they would come and they would want me to pass on messages to people around me. I remember being stood in line at the Pharmacy one day and a spirit came to me for the lady who was stood in front of me. They wanted me to tell her Auntie Ruby misses her and I told them no! Can you imagine me approaching someone in a place like that and passing on that kind of information? They would think I am seriously crazy. In the beginning I would tell people everything but I have also been bitten by the 'not everyone is a believer bug' and refuse to do that again. Of course I am respectful of the spirit and explained why but Auntie Ruby or whoever she was didn't stick around long enough to listen to me? I am pleased to say that through Nanna's advice I did manage to tune into them when I wanted, this did take some serious training but sometimes I think I did it too well because when I really need them at times they don't come. Of course the only real time I would try and channel them through would be when I was performing a psychic reading but back then readings were few and far between because of my full time job. That was until I opened the store anyway. I always know when a spirit is with me though because either they will give me a symptom of how they passed over such as pains in my chest, heart attack etc or other times they have given me a smell that only the person I am reading for will be able to understand. One of the most frustrating parts of doing what I do is that I can never guarantee who comes through and I try and make a joke out of that by saying to my clients 'this isn't Tesco's Supermarket, they don't come over the counter'. This does bring a smile to their faces but I still see the look of disappointment on their faces as they leave if they haven't managed to receive contact from the family member of their choice. On more than one occasion I have also had to bring spirits through that the person I'm reading for doesn't want to communicate with for whatever reason? The majority of the time it's due to quarrels or past arguments before the person passed away. What most people don't understand is that once a person has crossed over into the light they let go of any past hurt or personal emotional pain they experienced on the earth plane and as much as they are considerate to the human beings left behind, it's hard for them not to try and at least contact or speak to them at any opportunity they can.

I remember when my Nanna first passed over, I felt her around me a lot but as time progressed she only came when I truly needed her. I'm sure they have things they need to tend to on the other side; one day I will find out I'm sure. I can't see me going to hell somehow can you? There have been too many times in my life when spirits have come to me with messages for either me or a specific family member, the great thing about this is that by now the whole family knew I had the gift and would welcome the news from me. It's interesting how things have changed and how history seems to repeat itself with family. I always dreamed of being like my Nanna O'Conner, only I never for one-minute thought that would become a possibility? Back in the day when Nanna used to practice it was all done behind closed doors and passing of any silver from one hand to another was never spoken of but it did take place. I wish I could find out what Nanna thought of my store today, I'm sure she would be ever so proud of us and would no doubt be telling the world it was one of her grand daughters shop. I sometimes wish I could run ideas by her but all I need to do is ask for answers in my sleep and for some miraculous reason I always either wake up the idea or it comes to me throughout the day. I guess I am very blessed in that sense. I always try and use my spiritual connection for the good. Sometimes I lay in bed at night with my eyes closed and I ask what will become of a certain situation and before I know it I am taken to the exact scene in question and it's like as if I have a movie playing before my very eyes, it's quite bizarre but it will show me faces, scenarios, outcomes and all sorts. The best time for this is when I am exhausted and my body has just sunk into the bed because what I get shown then is actually in color whereas most times its blackened out and I have to dismantle the people I'm seeing if you will. Strange? Probably nothing is strange for you now after reading this? Let's just say we are 'different'. Now. I'm sure you can imagine this but since the store has been open we have attracted some of the strangest characters around. I have believe it or not through word of mouth managed to build a clientele from as far as Australia, Spain, America, Greece, France and many different cities throughout the UK. Like anything it hasn't been easy but I have managed to create a buzz that has intrigued people to come into the store. I went to a breakfast networking event and there was a lady there that has a client in North Wales; which is approximately four hours drive away from where we are in Swansea and even she has heard about our readings. I love this kind of success story because on the days where we may be quiet in the store we just have to remind ourselves that someone somewhere out there is talking about us. We all know that with any business the best form of advertising is word of mouth.

KICK START THE BROOMSTICK

Looking back on my past life as I like to call it, part of my role would be the 'New Developments' where I would go on site, oversee the whole project and remain there until the official launch party. I liked it because it always kept me on my toes. I can honestly say that I truly did think that I would have become bored by now with the store; I don't mean of the concept, I mean of actually staying in one place but I am pleasantly surprised to find that I'm not. Even on quiet days there is always something to be done and besides, it gives me time to plot the next big project. I think the hardest thing for me throughout this whole transition was having to deal with missing Sooty. There wasn't a day that went by without me crying and pining for him. All I could think was that he was just as sad as I was. Of course I knew he wasn't, he was probably loving every minute he spent at Janet's with Prada but I wish I could read into their thoughts at times, it would most certainly help to reassure us at times like that don't you think. I think this will be on the top of my list of questions when I enter the pearly gates; 'why can't we communicate with animals'? I guess I've always been the curious type really. I find myself searching for things that have no idea why or what for? Weird really I know but it does come in handy if I've lost something. My gift has always helped me to find missing items etc. I remember mum calling me in Miami one day to see if I could help her find their passports, I was shown in my head a drawer and the passports were placed in a brown envelope inside this drawer and right enough she went straight to the drawer and inside were the passports! Don't ask me how I know these things I just do. I think having a photographic memory most certainly helps because it allows me to play personal 'reminder movies' as I like to call them to help assist me.

The day came when I could fly Sooty to the U.K. My mum once again came to my rescue and made the journey up to Heathrow with me. Janet had arranged to get him all sorted on her end and the poor little thing was placed inside a plastic carrier and handed over to customs. Janet told him a little white lie and said that she would see him in half an hour only she didn't? She felt ever so guilty afterwards. We arrived to the counter and found out he had arrived safely yet he was missing some crucial signatures and until they received these from the vet in the US he would have to remain in quarantine. I am going out of my mind at this stage as you can imagine. We had just driven three hours to London to collect him; I had arranged coverage for the business also and there was just no way on this planet could I possibly drive back up there three days later. We sat there on pins for close to eight hours not knowing what was going on behind closed doors. I was texting and calling Janet, she was in work so it was really difficult to make things happen. I felt ever so guilty about putting all of this pressure on her but there truly wasn't much I could do about it. Eventually they found the missing paperwork; the container he was in had a cushion and within that cushion was a waterproof compartment where all of his paperwork was being held. Even after they managed to find the paperwork they needed they still had some concerns so by the time they finally agreed to let him go I was so nervous for him coming out; I didn't think he would have remembered me somehow and so I sprayed my perfume all over me. As soon as he came out he just looked so lovely and fluffy and ran straight towards me. He wouldn't stop kissing me bless him and smelling me. Of course I hadn't seen him for almost seven months so he was bound to be somewhat nervous around me but I think he knew that I was his mummy. What completely sealed the deal was when I went to pull the car up at the side of the building. I have the exact same car in this country as I had in the US, a little black mini convertible and as soon as he saw the car he went absolutely nuts!

KICK START THE BROOMSTICK

As soon as I opened the door he jumped straight in and sat in the passenger seat. It was adorable to see and then as soon as I sat in the car he wanted to be on my lap. In the US it is actually allowed so I waited until we got onto the M4 and he slept on my lap the whole way home. We stopped once on the journey down and he was absolutely fantastic. I was half expecting him to get carsick because he always did when we were in Miami but he was great. We arrived back in Swansea only now it was the biggest testing period of all. He needed to adjust to a whole new apartment. He had been living with Janet for the past seven months in a house and now he had to get used to an apartment again. Only this time it was going to be the cold weather he needed to adjust too also. The first night I allowed him to sleep on my bed with me, only because I could feel how nervous he was bless him. He was shaking and followed me around everywhere I went inside the apartment. The next morning of course I had to go to work and was very dubious about leaving him on his own but didn't really have a choice. I popped up in the day to check up on him and I'm glad I did; he was physically shaking profusely. I immediately panicked as you can imagine and just tried my best to comfort him. He was obviously scared and unsure of his surroundings. Clearly he was missing Prada, they've just spent every day together for the past seven months and now here he is all alone in a strange country in a strange apartment? I kept filling up with tears each time I looked at him. I have to say it did hurt because I thought perhaps he didn't remember who I was but that wasn't the case. He just had to get used to me being in his life again and vice versa! Like anything, it took its time and I continued to bring him to the shop for probably the first month until he was settled.

CHAPTER 18

The Magical Music Box

Not sure if you remember me telling you about Nanna O'Conner's magical musical jewelry box? Nanna always explained to us girls that if we ever needed to reach her or needed her help with anything all we would need to do is listen for the music of the box and she would be with us but this always worked in two different ways. If ever we heard the sound of the box for no apparent reason it meant that us three girls, Donna, Allison and myself were to meet immediately. The sound could only be heard by us girls in the beginning but then as we got older so the sound became noticeable to the people closest to us. i.e. husbands and boyfriends. Now, as you can imagine this could happen at any given time or place. Sometimes you were able to just deal with it and run to the meeting point or sometimes it was just plain and simple awkward! The meeting place changed each time depending on where we all were at the time but once the shop had opened this became the heart of what we did. Nanna would use this more to warn us of situations that were pending or to give us a heads up on people she could see coming in to the store and what she felt we could do to help them. Alternatively we would ask for her help and hope that she would hear our cry. Nine times out of ten she would try and come to our rescue but if there were situations that she felt we should handle ourselves then she wouldn't. The music would also play around us if ever we were in danger. When my store first opened, believe it or not I somehow managed to acquire a few stalkers along the way. Two of them I hadn't even met. One of the few mistakes I made moving back home was actually living on top of the store. In hindsight, looking back it was the perfect solution for me. No commute to work, local to the family. Close to a park for the dog and just overall very convenient. Unfortunately my store attracted some very different types of people. The first stalker I had had never met me. He was interested in one of the services we offered in the store and had initially just called to ask for information about it. Over the next few days he continued to call asking me questions; which I didn't mind to begin with but then the last time he called he claimed he was 'In-Love' with me? How could you possibly be in love with someone you have never met before? Of course I hung up the phone immediately and dialed 1471 to trace his number. It didn't end there though unfortunately, on two separate occasions I was walking through the car park at the side of the building and a man driving a very old clapped up banger of a car was sat watching me? He wound his window down and asked me what was the name of my dog. I instantly heard the music and I stopped in my tracks and pretended I hadn't heard him. My stomach just did a somersault; it completely flipped. I walked back in to the store and began to shake. What Nanna was trying to tell me was it was the voice from the phone calls. He had now resorted to watching me and therefore knew exactly where I lived. The music was with me all day that day but then he stopped contacting me for a few days until one day he called the store and asked to speak to me again, only to tell me that what I was wearing that day was pretty. This was the last straw; I had to go to the police. I had no choice. This man was clearly watching my every move. At the time Derek had just visited me and I explained what had happened. He had a friend of his call this man and gave him some friendly advice to leave me alone. Whatever was said worked because I never saw or heard from him again. I continued to have two more stalkers after this. Each one came with a warning from Nanna. I guess we were kind of lucky to have that but then other times it could be quite inconvenient.

I of course wasn't the only one. Both Donna and Allison had experienced this. Sometimes it can be hard to decipher the messages that are being given to us. Allison is a prime example of this. For months before Simon passed away she would dream about hearing the song and found herself now being able to understand what the message was about. Looking back now, it's absolutely as clear as day that Nanna was trying to protect her and give her support during the worst time of her life. This was very frustrating for Allison because at the time she thought she was imagining hearing the music. She was under the impression that we would only ever hear it together yet she couldn't understand why she found herself humming to the song and Donna and I didn't hear a thing. This message was for her only and therefore we wouldn't hear it. It wasn't until after Simon passed away that she told us what had been happening. Now she will always stop and try to analyze what is going on around her as soon as she hears it. The rule of thumb with the three of us is if we do hear it we have to text to see if it has come to the three of us, if it has then we arrange to meet at the store. If only one of us hear it we have to pay close attention to what is going on around us. I seem to hear the warnings the most but I think that is due to the fact the store attracts some weird characters. So much so that I have actually pretended before now that the store is closing just to get them out.

A gentleman came into the store once with what they call a

KICK START THE BROOMSTICK

'Dowser'. This can detect many different energy points surrounding you and also allow you to banish them easier. As I've already explained there are many ways to practice but this isn't one of my favorites. Anyway this man walked into the store and was mumbling under his breath and didn't even ask me if he could perform the cleansing he just started. I knew at the time he was practicing and actually leaving some kind of verbal spell because it almost looked as if his eyes were rolling in the back of his head? This man had very powerful sources working on his behalf, so much so that I couldn't even hear the music from Nanna. All I could see was Donna and Allison running into the store. They knew I was in trouble because I had failed to respond to their text and all Donna was told from the spirits was 'the baby needs you'. That's me! Donna is the toughest one out of the three of us and she asked me to go into the back room to drink some water. Her and Allison then asked this man kindly to leave the store but they could both feel how strong his magic was. In order for us to take care of him we needed the 'Power of Three'. I came back onto the storefront and we linked through our little fingers with our prayer and protection bracelets around our wrists and said the famous words 'Power of Three come to me, let us banish this magic in time for thee'. Within seconds it was like as if a different person was stood in front of us? This man asked if we were the Travel Agents two doors down? We said 'no' and so he apologized and left? Oh boy, was I thankful to my sisters that day. I wasn't thankful for the headache it left me with but once again, it comes with the territory.

It's funny how often the signs come. The last time I received a personal message was when I realized things were becoming strange with Derek again. My gut feeling was something was really wrong. The more contact I had with him and the longer I was home the more I got to see a completely different side to him. He just seemed to come across as being quite cocky and arrogant to a point of annoyance and surprise really and then the contact became less and less. I'm not going to lie to you. This truly did shock me. I guess when we first reconnected after all those years apart I thought things would have been different and something was, unfortunately he was. He was not the same person I knew all those years prior. The person I knew was almost humbled by his success. This person was almost expectant of people to bend over backwards for him and the only person he truly cared about was himself? He had absolutely no consideration for anyone else around him. Something in my heart just didn't feel right and as much as I tried to deny it I knew things were changing between us. You see, we've both changed, some things for the better but there are still certain traits he carried that I just resented. There was no way of getting around it, he was still this same selfish person underneath everything that he had been for last twenty years. Only now, it's just not good enough for me. I want the fairy tale still. I want to be the most important thing in someone's life. I want to be treated with respect as a person, not a thing? I want to be loved unconditionally. I want to have children one day. I don't think he can give me those things. Not only that, I think the longer this went on I can't honestly say I didn't even like him as a person anymore. Maybe I'm wrong to judge things but I can't really help it in this situation. We all know I eat, breath and sleep 'FATE' and still truly believe that my 'Knight in Shining Armor' is not far away, he's just fallen off his horse? There is someone our there for me its just all about timing and the way I look at it is I needed to go through this reunion with Derek to truly see that there was no future there. I guess I really did need to lay my ghosts to rest before I could truly find love. I'm glad actually that I experienced what I did over the past year because who knows I could have been sat around waiting for another twenty years. You have to admit though, it would have been the perfect fairy tale ending to my story only he is not my knight, I know that now. It might have taken me a very long time to see that but I have finally come to terms with it and believe it or not I am quite excited about the thought of meeting someone new. If I look back at past relationships I have been in I have always held something back from them, purely because Derek still had the key to that piece but now I feel completely different. I am actually looking forward to being able to give myself 100% to someone. I'm not sure what it's going to feel like but all I know is that I want to try. Let's see what the Universe brings me now that I have made this decision. I feel very proud of how I handled things; it just goes to show that time truly is a great healer. Writing this book has also allowed me to express my feelings and frustrations in a way I never thought I could. It's actually allowed me to lay a lot of ghosts to rest and now the future is mine to do what I want with. How exciting is that? O.K, now I'm rambling again!

Donna seems to hear Nanna's music with work situations. Each and every time she needs to make a decision she hears the music and follows her heart. She's never been wrong to this day. The most significant times she has heard the music is when she has made predictions. I remember on two separate occasions Donna had called me on my cell phone in Miami. The first time she called it was to look up any natural disasters around the world on the Internet. Donna had heard the music in her dreams and had visions of what she could only describe as paradise, white sandy beaches and clear sky blue Ocean. The problem she had with the vision was there was a house in front of her and as she stood at the front door of the house she was in paradise but as she entered the house and walked out the back door it was devastation and destruction? There were floodwaters close to four feet high, toys and dolls floating with the gushing waters and bodies and babies face down as if they'd drowned? Donna was absolutely devastated on the phone and could not calm down. Can you imagine having this kind of vision, it would distress to the strongest of people. I placed her on loudspeaker whilst I researched it on the web, but to no avail? The only thing that resembled somewhat of what she had seen was a landslide in the Dominican Republic, which a minor earthquake had caused. This couldn't be it but there really wasn't any other explanation that I could find. This was extremely frustrating for us because until we can identify what the message is from Nanna the music continues to play.

> Winds in the east, there's a mist coming' in
> Like something' is brewing' and 'about to begin.
> Can't put me finger on what lies in store,
> But I feel what's to happen all happened before.
> A father, a mother, a daughter a son
> The threads of their lives unraveling undone
> Something' is needed to twist 'them as tight,
> like string you might use when you're flying' a kite
> Chim chimeny chim chim, cheree chim cheroo!

It wasn't until two days later did we understand what Donna's message was. The Tsunami hit in the Pacific and caused destruction and devastation around the world. Almost 228,000 people lost their lives during this natural disaster. As you can imagine Donna and I spoke immediately as the news hit and could honestly say that this was in actual fact what she had seen. Donna really struggled to come to terms with this because she felt as though she had failed in her role somehow but we could never have known this was what she saw. It took us both quite a while to come to terms with it; we didn't speak for a few days because we just didn't know what to say to each other. Donna just kept crying all the time with guilt. Another time that stands out in our memory the same haunting way is when once again Donna called me to see if I could research a plane crash only I was in Finland at the time setting up a new Cruise Ship from the shipyard and so it was hard for me to gain access to the web. Donna had the Internet at home but didn't feel comfortable searching at the time. It's hard for you to understand the vibes we get and sometimes it scares us at the thought of what we would find. On this specific occasion the music was super strong around her and the only vision the spirits would give her is one of a small airplane that had crashed into her daughter Ashleigh's bedroom window? This was very disturbing for her as you can imagine and the worst thoughts were running through her head but once again there was nothing to be found on the web. I remember calling my dad to see if he could pick up on anything also but we were all left with a very unusual blank feeling in our bodies but not even dad could have imagined what happened next.

September 11th 2001 America was hit with the worst terrorist attack ever imaginable. As sad and crazy as this sounds, as soon as both planes hit the twin towers in New York City Donna burst into tears. This was once again exactly the vision she had been given by the spirits. How can anyone come to terms with something like this, knowing you could have perhaps prevented it? Truth is there was once again absolutely no way of knowing how to handle this prediction. Donna had no way of passing on her predictions to the world, and who would have believed her anyway? Where on earth would we begin to go with information like this? As much as it is wonderful to have the gift as we do, you can also see the downside to it now. The only way we move on from this is we also truly believe there is certain things we are not meant to know and therefore have to live with it. Not all of what we do has downsides. The majority of predictions we give can be extremely rewarding, especially when the clients come back into the store to advise us when things start happening in their world following their reading. 675 clients have either left messages in our 'Guest Comment Book' or have come specifically back into the store to give us feedback; which is the best compliment we could possibly receive. I love it more when the skeptics come in and are pretty much eating humble pie because they truly didn't believe the predictions when they left the store but are blown away when things start falling into place in their lives. I love to see the newborn babies we predicted, some surprises and some planned ha! The clients that have lost all hope in finding the love of their life suddenly took a different drive to work or tried a different supermarket for a change or tried a different network of friends, only to find Mr. or Mrs. Right in front of them. I have even had clients bring their new partner into the store to meet me and to say 'thank you' for helping to change their life for the better? The clients that have lost their jobs throughout the recession and for love or money can't seem to find a new one but most importantly have completely lost hope in finding one then all of a sudden there is a light at the end of the tunnel from their reading. Not only do we try and provide timing with the predictions we try and tune into whether the new job will be something they have done before or something completely new. I love reading for the men though. The majority of them that come into the store are pretty skeptical to say the least but I absolutely love it when I either get a phone call, text or email from them following their reading to say thank you, not only to let me know the predictions were pretty accurate but to advise me that things worked out bigger and better than they imagined. This is the part of my job that I absolutely adore. It gives me great satisfaction knowing that I have given someone hope.

Hope can come in many different ways. I have two specific stories I want to tell you about. The first is a regular client of mine who we shall call Angel, you'll understand why soon. Angel has been to me on several occasions only this time was different. She had lost a loved one very close to her and was struggling to come to terms with it. He was very young when he passed away and it had only been a week since he passed. I was unsure if he would even come to me at this stage as it was so soon. Normally it takes the spirit a few days, sometimes weeks to truly settle and come to terms with passing over but not this kid; he was as strong as an Ox and passed over such valuable information to Angel it was quite surprising, even to me. I don't think there were any tissues left in the box after she left bless her. The spirits were lined up to chat to her. My guess was that she was in such despair following his passing that they all came to her rescue and by the time we had finished her reading she left the store laughing at some of the stories and memories her relatives had shared with her. I absolutely love it when this happens and wish I could bring messages to every client I read for but unfortunately that's just not the case.

Sometimes messages maybe passed on to my clients with sadness. One lady that sticks to mind, we will call her Faith for privacy reasons. Faith had once again been to me several times before and there wasn't much of a stopgap in her last reading to this one. As soon as she walked into my room I wanted to burst into tears. Now when this happens I have to stop what I'm doing and ask the client if in actual fact there are tears with them because if I don't the emotion doesn't leave me as I explained earlier. I was right; she began crying uncontrollably and then we could see what had happened. The last time she came to me I told her that the relationship she was in was going to be over and that one of them would be walking away from the other; I couldn't see how or which one it was; it was confusing for me at the time. Faith told me that on the 30th of the month I gave her as a prediction her partner committed suicide. I just went numb all over and within seconds of her telling me he contacted me from the other side. He gave me his initial and showed me the damage he had caused to the door in which he had hung himself from. He also wanted to apologize profusely to her for being such a violent tyrant in the physical world. For years Faith had undergone both mental and physical abuse from her partner and he wanted to say sorry. He knew he needed help at the time and yet was so proud refused too. He was so embarrassed by his behavior and hoped that one day in her heart she would be able to forgive him. I think Faith was blown away with her reading and all of a sudden the overwhelming sense of grief had started to lift. Her reading for the future was actually very inspirational and believe it or not there was a new love to come into her life only this time she would be able to truly be herself and not hide behind the emotions or scared of the repercussions should she not comply to her partners wishes. I have to tell you, this was a very trying reading for me to do. It was extremely hard for me to be empathetic to her and yet struggle to not try and kick his ass in the spirit world for the abuse he put her through. I wanted to reach out to my brother and get him to kick his ass in heaven but I guess it doesn't work that way. Not only that, I have to keep my personal feelings to one side and not get emotionally involved or pass on my personal opinions. For those of you reading this that know me personally, I find this hard to do but I will say doing this job for a living has completely changed me in my approach to certain things. It's not about me at all; it's about the person sitting opposite me receiving the information I share with them. Sometimes they like what they hear, sometimes they don't? Either way I try and deliver the message in a way they will find easy to take on board. Normally I can judge the person by their reaction or if they are super sensitive I can truly feel what they are experiencing in their heart; which immediately tells me to think about how I say what needs to be said.

I think the hardest times I've had to deal with over the past year is when spirits, especially family members are trying to communicate with me all at the same time or they have been waiting for me to finish with a client and they become impatient and so when I do finally allow them through they are pretty agitated. There's not much I can do about that unfortunately. Like I keep saying 'this is not Tesco's; spirits don't come over the counter and as much as I would like to be alert to everyone that comes into my store it's just impossible to catch each and every one. Sometimes I'm glad I didn't speak with them, especially if they are not the nice kind. Over the past few weeks I have felt yet another strange energy around me; only this time it kind of felt familiar to me in a scary way though and I wasn't sure how? Something about the smell of it made me feel nervous inside. I've been trying to reach out to Nanna for the past few weeks to see if she could help me also because what ever it is, whoever it is has stopped people from entering into my store so I'm trying to do some investigating and hopefully by the time I finish the book I will have some answers for you.

CHAPTER 19

Where are they now?

So much has happened since we started the book that this may actually go on a little. Let's start at the top of the table as usual with Dad. This past year has been trying for him to say the least. Coming to terms with losing my brother has been difficult for both my parents. Dad is not getting any younger and you can see that in his face each time I see him. His health hasn't been the best but he is at least getting by. He still manages to annoy mum on a daily basis and yet they still kiss and make up. They are constantly taking off on vacation to Australia, Spain, Turkey and Portugal and lord only knows where they will end up next? Unfortunately Dad and the family were hit with more tragedy, his youngest brother my Uncle Malcolm passed away in September 2010 of a massive heart attack. This came as such a surprise to the whole family; he wasn't even ill? We were all so shocked and upset for our cousins because you see, the year prior to my brother passing away our Aunty Irene passed away with lung cancer; she was Uncle Malcolm's wife. The funeral was wonderful though; he truly did have a special send off and the boys seem to be coping well without him in their life. They didn't really have a choice. I think this made my dad do a lot of soul searching. You could see the tears in his eyes yet he tried to be strong for all of us. He still likes to do his usual thing and place a little bet on the horses every day. Mum likes the Bingo so why not? One thing that has changed for me is that when I lived in the US I always had my one on one phone call with him and we would speak for almost an hour at times but those are very few and far between now. I need to make more of an effort with it though I know but I do miss that special time we had.

As for Mum, well she is still struggling with her health. She is still recovering from the cancer and yet is struggling more than anything. She has been in and out of hospital with everything from tummy problems to general aches and pains to a point where she is just exhausted by it all now. I hate seeing my mum cry; it just breaks my heart but we just have to be there for her. All of the tests have come back negative so far; which is a great thing but she is still convinced something is not right. She's not being paranoid; she just keeps saying that her bones are aching all the time. They have finally just recently run some tests and so we have to wait for the results to come back. Hopefully she will get some clarity then also. Mum still cries over Terry to this day. It's so hard for her, especially now since Lauren, Terry's eldest daughter has recently given birth to a little boy called Jayden. This pregnancy wasn't exactly well received. You see, Lauren is only fifteen years of age and is still just a baby herself. We were all really worried about her having a child at such a young age and especially seen as she has been a bit of a rebel up until now. None of us knew what to expect but Kelly told her at the time that if she wanted to keep the child she could and so she did. This pregnancy has put a tremendous amount of pressure on both my parents, especially mum. She has pretty much spent a small fortune on Lauren and the baby but as she said, my brother isn't here to help her. I know this kind of sounds pretty selfish of me to say this but she just doesn't need added stress. Stress is one of the most recognized causes of cancer to return in the body; this is the last thing she needs. Mum will always be mum and won't ever stop trying to conquer the world or the family's problems one at a time. It's strange though because personally I think she looks lovely at the moment. I know she's frustrated to the high heavens though and will be glad once all of the results come back. I'm just glad I'm home, even if I do only get to see her and dad perhaps once a week sometimes, it's more than I ever have for the past twenty years. Fingers crossed now she will start to recover and enjoy the rest of her life. We are all hoping she moves to a bungalow soon though; the apartment where they live is up a flight of stairs and it's now beginning to take its toll on both her and dad with their age.

Donna Wonna is still Donna Wonna. Working her butt off as usual to give Ben and Ashleigh whatever they want. Ben has recently started an IT course College and is quite excited with it. Ashleigh is still the same, loving boys only now she has a boyfriend called Tim. He seems like a lovely person. Donna is still working hard trying to secure her Senior Management Position with Social Services but with the deficit the company is in they have made cut backs to Management roles and she will be reverting back to her old location and position at the beginning of next month. I'm gutted for her actually and hope that she get's a really fantastic break and soon. I wish my store was busy enough for the both of us with readings. I would love her to pack in her full time job and come work with me but at this moment in time its just not possible. I know any new business takes its time to grow and that's where I am at the moment but as soon as I get the opportunity to expand to a 2nd location then I will most certainly consider using her more. Both her and Allison are still supporting me with special events and things like that. We have such great fun when we do them. So fingers crossed the book will be a huge success and then the sky will be the limit for us. Allison on the other hand has also had lots of changes.

KICK START THE BROOMSTICK

Firstly she has changed her job from the Housekeeping and Kitchen part of the company into the caring field of work. The only problem with this is that she now has to work shifts; which has kind of dampened her social life a bit. On the brighter side of this though she has started to spend time with new friends and has been venturing into the City on girls nights out where she hopes to meet a very special someone. I am keeping my fingers and toes crossed for her that she does. Every time we do the Tarot Cards for her it tells me someone is coming back into her life from her past? It's quite confusing actually because it's been telling us the same thing for a year? We are still waiting for this to happen so we will keep you updated as and when things transpire with her. The girls are great. Sam has been spending lots of time with Kelly and the children. She is on her last year of school and wants to proceed into Nursing when she leaves next summer. I can't believe she is going to be sixteen soon? Charlotte and Pat are still very much in love. They are saving like mad at the moment to buy their first house. They work their little butts off bless them and have stopped socializing as much as they used to and haven't taken a vacation this year purely for that reason. Charlotte is still trying to find a way to enter into the beauty industry; however jobs are very few and far between. I keep looking through the jobsites daily to see if I can find something for her but it's hard at the moment. Again, I'm hoping things will improve here so that we can expand and add the Spa aspect to the business; she can manage it and put all of her years training into practice.

My brother's children are lovely all thanks to Kelly. They are growing up so big and have their very own special personalities. It's funny actually because when Terry was alive they were all so very different and now they are truly coming out of their shells. It's wonderful to see. Kelly is still having issues with Lauren. Her house just isn't big enough to house them and it's putting a lot of pressure on her when she just doesn't need it. Like everything else in our family, it will work itself out, it always does. Unfortunately Kelly had more sadness to deal with. Her Dad passed away in September 2010, so not only has she lost my brother but she has also lost both of her parents. Life is just such a shit at times isn't it? I just hope that Kelly is the next one in line to meet someone new. She is such a wonderful person that she deserves it. I would hate to see her lonely for the rest of her life, she's only 31! She can't see herself meeting anyone but for some unknown reason, every time I do her Tarot Cards it also states someone from her past is going to return. It also shows she will have a choice of men though so good luck there Kelly.

As for me, here I am busting my little butt in a job I adore. I love doing Psychic readings for people. I love my little store; I love everything about it. I do wish it were busier than it is but I know something very exciting is going to happen soon I can just feel it in my tummy. I've been trying to network as much as I possibly can to get the word out into the community and it's definitely working. My reputation through word of mouth has also grown. I guess it's taken the results of people I've read for over the past year to come to fruition for them to now promote the services we offer. Check us out on YouTube; I've been doing daily blogs promoting the store and other local businesses. I'm still enjoying being home in Wales even though I do still miss my friends in Miami. I've started dating again, something I never thought I would do and am quite happy. I've met someone extra special and pretty amazing. Let's see if he makes it to book No.2 and then you'll know how special he is! I actually think my life has changed in so many ways for the better. I find myself doing things I love to do but never had the time when I lived in Miami. The next stage of my journey is yet to be determined but for now I will enjoy the ride with my family and very special friends.

As for the store, remember me telling you that I felt some strange energy around it again over the past few weeks? A very old lady, a client of mine came in yesterday with a gift for me. She could see that I collected old Antique pieces and came across a piece she thought I might like? My stomach turned; I did not like the feeling the box was giving me and was actually dreading opening it. My hands started trembling, I felt sick and started sweating. Nancy asked if I was O.K and told me to sit down. As I did she dropped the box and what rolled out onto the floor…. The Henry VIII Toby Jug that I had thrown out week's prior. As soon as I saw it every light bulb in my store exploded and I ran to protect Nancy. As the glass shattered and fell to the floor, all I could hear was… 'I'm back, only this time for good'…